WIFE BATTERING IN CANADA: THE VICIOUS CIRCLE

BY
Linda MacLeod

assisted by
Andrée Cadieux

January 1980

Prepared for the
Canadian Advisory Council
on the Status of Women
151 Sparks Street
Box 1541, Station B
Ottawa, Ontario
K1P 5R5

Cette édition est aussi disponible en français.

©Minister of Supply and Services Canada 1980
Available in Canada through
Authorized Bookstore Agents and other bookstores
or by mail from

Canadian Government Publishing Centre
Supply and Services Canada
Hull, Quebec, Canada K1A 0S9

Catalogue No. LW31-4/1980   Canada: **$2.95**
ISBN 0-660-10483-0   Other countries: **$3.55**

Price subject to change without notice.

1

TABLE OF CONTENTS

CHAPTER I

WIFE BATTERING CAN HAPPEN IN YOUR FAMILY

[1] For the sake of the women and their families, some of the details in these case histories have been changed.

Karen W.[1]

Karen was just 14 when she met Richard. He came with his family to one of her parents' summer barbeques. He was 19, a journeyman electrician, working in the construction business, as did both their fathers. Karen's father liked him immediately. It wasn't every young man nowadays who would stick through an apprenticeship with the long hours and low pay. He himself had apprenticed as a bricklayer, and now he owned his own construction firm. Rich looked like a young man who could do the same thing.

Rich came often to the house after that, becoming a part of the family activities. It was easy enough to set another place at the table with Karen and her five brothers and sisters.

By the time she was fifteen, Karen and Rich were 'going steady'. Most of their social life was with Karen's sisters and brothers, and it was generally a happy time. Occasionally, when there were other boys from Karen's school included, Rich would become moody and silent. He said they were immature, and he made her promise she wouldn't pay any attention to them. He talked about getting married as soon as Karen was old enough. Plans became more specific; they were to be married soon after Karen's 17th birthday.

It was a huge wedding. Karen looked beautiful, her parents were pleased. Rich was hardworking, he was Catholic. They weren't particularly concerned that she hadn't finished high school; she would be getting married anyway, and certainly materially she would never want for anything.

They began their married life in the three-bedroom house that Karen's parents had given them for a wedding present. Within three months she was pregnant. It was soon after this, after a party at her sister's, that they arrived home and no sooner had the door closed than Rich suddenly viciously punched her in the face. She reeled back in horror and surprise. He accused her of flirting with her brother-in-law - suggested she had probably been carrying on an affair with him. She denied this and he hit her again. She locked herself in the bathroom until she heard him go to bed. She spent the night on the living room chesterfield. She told no one. The beatings continued. At the same time, she and Rich continued to take part in all the activities of her large, warm family. Her first baby, a girl, was born, and 14 months later, a boy. There were baptism parties; the family went to mass together; in summer they went to the lake for family picnics. Karen, ashamed, told her parents nothing of the beatings. When the bruises couldn't be hidden by sunglasses or high-necked sweaters, both she and her husband would lie about them.

When finally he threatened to kill her or her baby daughter, she tried to tell her parents. They wouldn't believe her. Such things didn't happen. She was exaggerating. She should just go on being as good a wife and mother as she could, and everything would be alright. One day she heard a staff member from a transition house for women who have been battered being interviewed on the radio. Four days later Rich beat her up again. The next day, after he had gone to work, she packed up the children and went to the house. She had been married five years. She had bruises on her face, neck and abdomen. Finally her parents were forced to face the fact that something terrible had been happening. They were very supportive of her decision to get a separation agreement. Her husband was ordered by the courts to keep the peace. Karen's father persuaded him to leave the house, and had the locks changed.

Karen stayed at the transition house for three weeks while she went through the court process. During that time she met with a counsellor from the community college, and discussed, with growing excitement, the possibilities for further education. Before she left the transition house she had enrolled for the coming term in an upgrading program to complete her high school. Day care would be provided by the college, and her parents would support her until she was self-sufficient.

Two weeks after she had returned to her home, Rich broke in, locked the two children in the bedroom, beat Karen, and finally shot her. He then went into the basement and hanged himself. That was how Karen's father found them all when he dropped by two days later for a casual visit.

Susan A.

Susan had been a pretty, quiet, studious English major. After graduation she took a job writing advertisements for a department store. She met Gary, an outgoing extroverted sales representative for an appliance company. He was full of energy, a lot of fun; he knew where all the exciting places were, and he seemed to have hundreds of friends. He loved a party; maybe he drank a bit too much, but he always had a good time. She was 22 when they got married. She gladly quit her job right away, because Gary wanted her to be a full-time wife. Their first child was born within a year. The violence started almost at the beginning. She had tried to overlook it, had forgiven him, because she knew his job put him under a lot of pressure, and he would have a few drinks to relax. He would never hit her, she was sure, if he wasn't drinking. A second child was born. Finally the situation was too much; she tried to leave, as she was to try several times over the next few years. Each time he would persuade her to give him another chance, he would promise to reform. Two more children were born. Gary was promoted to sales manager; the pay was higher but Gary, who was not comfortable in a managerial job, was under even more strain. Occasionally Gary would have to stay home because of his drinking, but he was a good salesman and a good provider. They looked like the perfect family in their split-level suburban home with its outdoor swimming pool. When the youngest child was in nursery school Susan got a clerical job and prepared the way to leave eventually. The beatings continued. Finally, on one occasion the oldest child, Lori, tried to intervene, and Gary beat her up too. Susan took the children and left. She found herself an apartment, bought a second-hand car. Lori looked after the younger children after school until her mother got home.

She had not told Gary where she was, but he found out easily enough by simply phoning the company where she worked. He came one day while she was still at work and persuaded the youngest child, Kenny, to let him in. When Susan returned home he beat her, and Lori as well. Susan called the police and laid an assault charge, but she realized she was no longer safe in the apartment. She and the children moved into a transition house until she could earn enough money to pay the first and last month's rent on another apartment.

Staff at the transition house noted that the youngest child was terrified if men came to the door. Gary was put on a peace bond - ordered by the court not to hit his wife again. Susan proceeded to get a separation agreement and interim custody of the children. However, as she drove into the parking lot at work one morning, Gary was waiting for her. He smashed the windshield in with a crowbar and attacked her. One eye was severely gouged, the other also injured, and she sustained a concussion. The terrified security guard called the police.

For three weeks there was some doubt as to whether or not Susan would lose an eye. Finally she recovered.

Gary was charged with attempted murder. When he finally came to court four months and several adjournments later, he was found guilty of assault causing bodily harm, and given a one-year suspended sentence. He has therefore spent a total of one day in jail for this crime - the day he was arrested.

Susan, her prettiness marred by a badly scarred left eye, continues to live on her own with her four children, supporting them on $904 per month. She is determined to make it without any help from anyone.

Wife Battering Must Come Out of the Closet

Wife battering is a fact of life in families across Canada. Women are kicked, punched, beaten, burned, threatened, knifed and shot, not by strangers who break into their houses or who accost them on dark streets, but by husbands and lovers they've spent many years with - years with good times as well as bad.

In every neighbourhood there are women who are battered by their husbands or live-in lovers. Wife battering crosses geographic and income lines. It is as common in rural households as in urban. It spans all ages, races and nationalities. In some families it is an isolated or occasional occurrence, but in others it is a daily routine.

Wife battering is, of course, not the only kind of family violence. We are all horrified at stories we read of child abuse and incest, and more recently cases of husband beating and "granny bashing" have come to public attention. While we have no conclusive statistics on "granny bashing", the number of families which include three generations are relatively rare. Child abuse is receiving widespread public attention and reporting of known child abuse cases by some citizens outside the family has become legally mandatory. Husband battering also does exist, but its existence relative to wife battering must be put in perspective. A number of studies on family violence have reported on this phenomenon and have concluded that:

> *The few women who resorted to counterviolence did so as an act of desperation associated with failure of other options.*[2]

While men are killed by their wives as well as women by their husbands,

> *long-term physical abuse between spouses is almost always perpetrated by the man.*[3]

and

> *If one uses injuries as a criterion, then wife-beating would far outdistance husband beating.*[4]

In other words, wife battering and husband battering are very different phenomena. The few women who inflict serious harm on their husbands usually do so for self-preservation, after enduring prolonged violence against themselves or their children.

Wife battering has not received the public attention it deserves. Too often it is explained away as atypical or as an individual aberration, and its seriousness is lightened by making it the subject of jokes. But wife battering is too serious to be laughed away and too common to be explained away as an "illness" or a "personal problem". Wife battering is much more than an individual dilemma or an occasional outburst. It is a way of life which touches us all indirectly or directly because it is perpetuated by our beliefs, traditions and institutions.

[2] Hilberman, Elaine, & Munson, Kit, *60 Battered Women*, p. 4. Prepared for American Psychological Association Meetings, Toronto, Ontario, May 5, 1977.

[3] Hamlin, Diane, *The Nature and Extent of Spouse Assault*, Center for Women Policy Studies, Clearinghouse Director, Washington, D.C., October 1978, p. 1

[4] Strauss, Murray, *Behind Closed Doors: Violence in the American Family*, Doubleday, N.Y. (to be released in 1980). Reported in the *Calgary Herald*, October 2, 1979.

What Is Wife Battering?

To clarify how wife battering will be used throughout this report, an operational definition will be offered which enumerates what wife battering is not as well as what it is.

Wife battering is not just the result of an isolated argument that has got out of hand. According to a British study of wife abuse, more than three-quarters of the women surveyed reported that physical assaults were usually not preceded by verbal arguments.[5] Neither is wife beating to be confused with sado-masochistic behaviour on the part of two consenting adults. It is not playful, fun, or sexually stimulating for the woman.[6]

Wife battering is not confined to legally married couples. It applies equally to couples in common-law marriages and to couples living together. It does not occur only in heterosexual couples - it can also refer to battering of the partner who adopts the "wife" role in a homosexual or lesbian relationship. The terms "wife," "husband" and "marriage" will, however, be used throughout largely for convenience and also as a reminder that the battering we are discussing cannot be separated from the family context, or from the "husband" and "wife" roles which can be just as strong inside or outside a legal marriage.

Wife battering is violence, physical and/or psychological, expressed by a husband or a male or lesbian live-in lover toward his wife or his/her live-in lover, to which the "wife" does not consent, and which is directly or indirectly condoned by the traditions, laws and attitudes prevalent in the society in which it occurs.

The violence women who are battered experience, is therefore a combination of three types of violence: physical violence, psychological violence directly initiated by their husbands in the form of constant denigration, taunts, purposeful inconsistencies or threats, and the psychological violence these women experience when they try to get help outside the family to stop the battering and find that help is too often just not there.

Women who are battered and look for help, learn very quickly that violence is an integral part, not just of certain family interactions, but of our whole society and that violence in the family is indirectly supported by practices and policies which condone some violence by husbands against wives.

From the first hand reports of women who have been battered, an experiential definition emerges which brings the three sides of wife battering to life. Being battered is feeling confused, feeling dead inside, feeling worthless, having no friends - not even one that you can call when you're feeling really low. It's not knowing when he'll turn on the kids - always feeling jumpy, never knowing when it will start again. It's being afraid all the time - not just of him but of everything - not really trusting anyone or anything. It's feeling guilty and in some indefinable way responsible, even though you're the one who's being beaten.

How This Study Was Done

Most of the facts for this report were gathered from groups and agencies taking an active role in the intervention/prevention of wife battering. Transition houses across Canada - houses where battered women and their children can stay temporarily for protection and support - and some hostels which accept battered wives - 73 in all[7] - were contacted and given in-depth telephone interviews on the process of wife battering. Barriers to effective help experienced

[5] Support Services for Assaulted Women. *Wife Assault in Canada - A Fact Sheet*, Toronto, Ontario.

[6] Carol Victor found in er survey of 80 battering cases that no wives who were battered desired sexual relations with their husbands after being beaten, although 18 husbands who committed the attacks did. Reported in Davidson, Terry, *Conjugal Crime*. p. 65-66

[7] Not all houses contacted were in operation at the time of this survey. Two had closed during 1979, but the former workers were contacted to discover why they had closed, to make use of their insights about wife battering and to include their 1978 statistics in our estimates.

by women who have been battered and obstacles that transition house workers encounter in providing effective support for these women were discussed. Transition house workers were also asked to send any statistics they had collected on the women who stayed at their houses, as well as any detailed reports or pamphlets they had prepared. Forty-seven houses did send statistics; the others, usually recently open, did not yet have an organized data collection system, because they had been open too short a time, or didn't have enough staff to include data collection in their duties.

In addition, provincial police departments were contacted, as were some local police departments (in randomly selected centres in each province), provincial family court offices, offices of attorneys-general, provincial social service offices, selected children's aid society offices and a few larger hospitals across Canada in an attempt to gather further statistical information on the subject.

Unfortunately this search proved virtually fruitless. Although all police departments were very cooperative, we found that they have figures on assaults but do not separate assault cases by sex of the victim or offender, or by the relation between them. None of the other services contacted collected statistics on wife battering in any systematic way.

The Focus of This Report

This report will emphasize the frustrations, dilemmas and barriers women experience when they make others aware that they have been battered. It will expose the incidence and characteristics of wife battering. It will examine common myths about wife battering as well as the legal, medical and counselling procedures which help perpetuate these myths. It will look at an image of the family, developed centuries ago, but still perpetuated by our laws and traditions, which places the family outside the law and reinforces the right of men to beat their wives. It will look less at the individual characteristics of "battered wives" and "battering husbands" but focus more on the social system which perpetuates and accepts wife battering throughout our society. Finally this report will look towards directions for change - change which will protect women from being battered, change which will revise procedures that leave women who have been battered with nowhere to turn, change that will enable people to live in families without violence.

CHAPTER II

WIFE BATTERING IS A FACT OF LIFE

Interpreting the Statistics

The statistics and insights presented in this chapter, except where otherwise indicated, are derived from the statistical reports submitted by transition houses and from the verbal information and case histories they offered. This is the first time an attempt has been made to collect national information on wife battering in Canada, using the largest identified sample available - those women who stay in transition houses for battered women and hostels which accept women who have been battered. The statistics give us much valuable information therefore, but should not be interpreted as describing all cases of wife battering in Canada. Much more research across classes and in rural as well as urban areas is still needed.

Annual statistics for 1978 were used whenever possible. Where figures for only part of 1978 were available, adjustments were made to approximate annual figures, assuming that month-to-month variations would not be significant. Some houses used more detailed questionnaires than others for their residents, and as a result not all information was available from all the houses. The number of houses that submitted information on each question discussed is therefore noted. Although the data presented is derived from different intake questionnaires and so is not standardized, it is generally recognized that even given this limitation,

> The best information available at the present time on the victims of spouse abuse is found in the writings of academics and professionals who are analyzing data obtained from residents of shelters.[8]

[8] Hamlin, Diane. *op. cit.*, p. 6.

Because the number of houses in each province is not proportional to the provincial population, and because the houses which submitted statistics were not evenly distributed across the country, no attempt is made to offer provincial breakdowns and figures are presented as proportions only, except in the approximations of incidence. U.S. and British studies and statistics have been used throughout the paper primarily to support Canadian studies and statistics, but occasionally they stand alone when no Canadian information was available.

Our findings follow.

The Facts Speak for Themselves

Battering is Rarely a One-Time Occurrence

Eight houses collected statistics on the regularity of beatings received by the women who stayed in the houses.

> **31% of transition house residents who were asked how regularly they were beaten, answered that they were beaten weekly or daily. 26% were beaten at least once a month.**

Three of the houses also asked their residents how many times in total they had been beaten before. One house reported that 84% of its residents had been beaten at least <u>eleven</u> times. The other two houses found that almost all their residents had been beaten many times before.

Beatings Are Frequently Severe

In about one-third of the cases, medical treatment was required and received.

Four houses queried their residents about medical treatment. Between 30% and 36% of the women asked, responded that they had required medical care.

An American study graphically describes the extent of injuries women receive. Out of a sample of 100 women,

> All had received the minimum of bruises, but 44 had also received lacerations of which 17 were due to attack with a sharp instrument such as a bottle, knife or razor. Twenty-six had received fractures of nose, teeth or ribs and eight had fractures of other bones, ranging from fingers and arms to jaw and skull. Two had their jaws dislocated and two others had similar injuries to the shoulder. There was evidence of retinal damage in two women and one had epilepsy as a result of her injuries. In 19 cases there were allegations that strangulation attempts had been made. Burns and scalds occurred in eleven and bites in seven cases. All women were attacked with the minimum of a clenched fist, but 59 claimed that kicking was a regular feature. In 42 cases, a weapon was used, usually the first available object, but in 15 cases this was the same object each time, eight being a belt with a buckle.[9]

Wife Batterings Do Become Homicides

Of 107 reported murders in immediate families in Canada in 1975, the wife was killed by the husband in 49 cases, but the husband was killed by the wife in only 8.[10]

No discussion of severity would be complete without a consideration of homicide - far too many men who beat their wives end up killing them. Of course, any estimate of the number of cases of wife battering that end in murder is bound to be low, since deaths resulting from family violence are frequently classified as "accidental", and we have no way of knowing, except through individual reports, how many cases result in suicides or slow deaths through illness or disability triggered by the beatings.

Two personal accounts document this kind of tragedy poignantly:

> I worked for a lady for 3 years; she was beaten repeatedly. Broken nose, hit behind her ear with a beer bottle and needed drainage on this injury for several years. Kicked in the seat, fell and injured, hop walked with a cane rest of her life, which ended in an insane asylum in B.C. My very best friend.

> This form covers abuse of two separate women who rented an apartment in my home at different times with common-law partners. One died in early 40's a few years ago. The other has been a patient in a psychiatric hospital for 6 or 7 years where she will probably remain the rest of her life (she is in her early 30's).[11]

Even the murders we can document, however, portray the magnitude of the danger women experience in their families. Between 1968 and 1974, 37.3% of all murder cases were reported as domestic and almost 11 out of 12 of these involved members of the immediate family, whether legally married or common-law.[12]

[9] Gayford, J.J., "Battered Wives" in Martin, J.P., ed., *Violence and the Family*, John Wiley and Sons, New York, 1978, p. 21-22.

[10] Goldman, Pearl. *Violence Against Women in the Family*, unpublished Master of Laws Thesis, McGill University, 1978, p. 11.

[11] Accounts quoted from *Women in Transition*, a Canada Works project, Thunder Bay, Ontario, 1978.

[12] Statistics Canada. *Homicide in Canada*, 1974, Cat. 85-505E.

If we look at all homicide victims in Canada between 1961 and 1974, 60% of all female victims were killed within a family context, more than double the proportion of male victims.

Physical beating as the direct cause of death is most prevalent in common-law family murders, where it accounts for 29.5% of these murders. Beating is the cause of death in only 16.9% of immediate family murders (i.e. murders in families where the spouses are legally married). Shooting is a much more common cause of death in family murders, accounting for 48.5% of immediate family deaths, 39.2% of common-law family deaths and 56.8% of lovers' quarrels.[13]

[13] Statistics Canada, op. cit., p. 28

We can conclude with complete surety from the above figures that wife battering led to at least 1/5 of husband/wife murders. But the actual figures are probably much higher, especially if we consider that wife battering can indirectly cause murders of husbands by their wives. In Chimbas' study of Ontario husband/wife homicides, all of the female offenders had been seriously assaulted by their victims.[14] To repeat a point introduced at the beginning of this report, female violence resulting in serious physical harm is almost always violence triggered by self-preservation.

[14] Support Services for Assaulted Women, op. cit.

Where and When Battering Occurs

70% of wife battering occurs between 5:00 p.m. and 7:00 a.m.

The questions of where and when battering occurs can be answered succinctly by saying: in private places and at private times, away from the prying eyes of neighbours, friends and any potential help for the victim.

Almost half of all battering, according to our statistics, occurs between 5 p.m. and 12 midnight. Another 15-20% occurs between 12 midnight and 7 a.m. About half the incidents occur on weekends, and most cases of family violence occur in the family home - the kitchen and "master" bedroom being the most dangerous rooms.

An Ontario Provincial police officer added that when domestic disputes occur outside the home, they usually take place where help is non-existent. Many cases occur in cars for instance. Wife battering which takes place in a car can rarely be proved, since the husband can claim his wife jumped or fell out of the car.[15]

[15] Telephone conversation with an Ontario Provincial Police officer, Toronto, October, 1979.

Wife Battering Does Not Happen Only in Cities

Unfortunately, transition houses are very difficult to establish in rural and isolated areas because of the distances between residents. It would be very difficult to make women in these areas aware of the existence of a transition house without also letting their husbands know of its location. The protection of the women who went to the house would thereby be jeopardized. However, we do know that despite these overwhelming problems, one of the transition houses and hostels we contacted is in a village with under 1,500 inhabitants, and another five are in towns with fewer than 15,000 people.

[16] Gelles, Richard, The Violent Home, Sage, Beverly Hills, California, 1972, p. 145.

[17] Steinmetz, Suzanne K., The Cycle of Violence: Assertive Aggressive and Abusive Family Interaction, Praeger, New York, 1977, p. 77.

Battering Often Occurs During Pregnancy

Only one house asked whether the woman was beaten during pregnancy, but 80% of these women answered positively. Gelles also found that 10 of the 44 women he interviewed reported being beaten when pregnant,[16] Steinmetz cites pregnancy as one of the major incitements to violence,[17] and Gayford identifies pregnancy as the factor which most often precipitates violence.[18]

[18] Gayford, J.J., "Battered Wives", in Martin, J.P., op. cit., p. 21.

11

Women Who Stayed in Transition Houses

Statistical Snapshot of Women Who Stayed in Transition Houses in 1978:

Age: 28
Married: 7 years
White
Works in the home
Annual Family Income: $10,000
Has left her husband once before.
Has 1 or 2 young children.
Was battered when pregnant.
Has Grade 11 education.

Warning: This "snapshot" is a statistical fabrication - an averaging of many very different family situations in which battering occurs. It must be remembered that this "snapshot" only describes in a very crude way women who stayed in transition houses in 1978. It is not a stereotyped portrait of all battered women since there is no typical case of wife battering, and the women who stay at transition houses do not represent all battered women, for a number of reasons:

1. The first reason has to do with regulations many of the houses must abide by to receive funding needed to operate their houses. More will be said about this problem in a later chapter, but in many houses women who have a source of income other than welfare and women without children cannot always be accepted if the house is to receive its full funding allotment.

2. Women in rural and isolated areas usually must travel many miles to a transition house, so transportation is costly and difficult to arrange. Also, because of their relative isolation, these women are less likely to receive information about the houses nearest to them.

3. Middle and upper-class women and older women regardless of their class are more reluctant to admit that they are battered - the stigma is perceived to be greater.

   There is such a stigma attached to this problem especially in the middle and upper class that the real need seems to be somewhere to get advice and counselling without a lot of red tape and publicity.[19]

   They are also more likely to think their situation is special. "Certainly nearly all the older battered wives were under the impression that their situation was unique."[20]

4. Women with money of their own can sometimes afford to go to a hotel, to hire a lawyer. The transition house is not their only option. It must not be assumed however that all middle and upper-class women or all working women regardless of their class have access to money. Frequently all family finances are controlled by the husband and at best the wife receives an allowance.

As a result, women from higher income groups and rural areas, women who work outside the home, women without children and older women tend to be under-represented in the figures which were used to create the "snapshot" above.

To present a more well-rounded picture, statistics detailing the range of characteristics of the residents are presented below. These statistics should be

[19] Comment from *Women in Transition*, op. cit.

[20] Gayford, J.J., "Battered Wives", in Martin, J.P., op. cit., p. 22.

12

seen as estimates only, since in some cases houses did not differentiate between residents who were battered and those who stayed at the house for other reasons.

Age

Of all the women who stayed in transition houses in 1978,
21% were under 20
39% were between 20 and 30
23% were between 30 and 40
17% were over 40.

Marital Status

62.3% of the women were legally married
24.2% lived in common-law relationships
The remainder were single, separated or divorced.

Length of Relationship

The average length of the marriage or common-law relationship for the women who stayed in the five transition houses which recorded this information ranged between five and eight years. Only one house collected statistics on the age at which the women married, but this house found that 45% married before they were 20, and another 32% between the ages of 20 and 25.

Employment Status

22% of the women worked outside the home. There were no figures available on whether they worked full-time or part-time.

Family Income

Only one house collected income figures and estimated the average annual income at $10,000.

Previous Separations

46% of the women in marriages or common-law relationships had left their husbands before. The one house which asked these women how many times they had left, found that 40% had left only once before, 22% had left twice and 38% had left their husbands three or more times.

Miscellaneous

Detailed statistics on education and number and ages of children were not available. Statistics on race tend to over-estimate the incidence of wife battering among native peoples since a statistic on race is usually only kept by houses with a large native clientele.

Other Canadian studies of transition house residents support these figures. Ken Menzies found that 45% of the women who came to Women's Emergency Centre in Woodstock between January 1976 and April 1977 were between 16 and 25, 28% 26-34 and 20% 35-44.[21] Chan, studying 194 women who were housed in "Women in Transition" in Toronto between 1974 and 1976, found that "there is a slight over-representation of relatively young married women...more than half of them range between twenty and thirty years of age...". Chan also found that more than half the children were between one and six years old, and the women had an average of 1.9 children.[22] He reported that only 26% of the women in the sample had Grade 11-13 education, and only

[21] Menzies, Ken, *The Women's Emergency Centre: An Assessment*, Department of Sociology and Anthropology, University of Guelph, 1977, p. 3.

[22] Chan, Kwok Bun, *Husband-Wife Violence in Toronto*, unpublished Ph.D. thesis, York University, Toronto, 1978, p. 3-4.

13

7% had attained schooling beyond Grade 13. Over half of the women had not worked for over five years, and only 17 had worked in the labour force within the six month period before they came to the transition house. "Thirty-six women were engaged in some kind of labour job while another 32 women took up the traditional low-paid clerical positions in commercial firms and factory offices."[23]

Gayford, in <u>Violence and the Family</u>, paints a similar picture. He concludes that although there was a wide age range, most women were still within the child-bearing age group.[24] Seven per cent of the women were never employed, 32% had worked in one job at least three years and the mean age of marriage or cohabitation was 20.3.[25]

Studies of battered wives which use statistical sources other than transition house data do find that the average age tends to be higher. A study in Windsor, Ontario, found that "the battered wife is, on average, 37 years of age, married more than ten years, the mother of several children and a homemaker".[26]

What Do We Know About Their Husbands?

We know that over 50% of the husbands of the battered women interviewed by transition houses had been beaten as children, compared to about one-third of the women. We know that 55% of the husbands were working, that the one house which asked whether the mate had a criminal record found that 34% did, and that the husband's educational level tended to be, like his wife's, about Grade 11.

Kwok Chan found that 25% of the mates of wives in his sample were unemployed, and the "other 75% were actually employed in the labour force. More than half of these men declared and identified themselves as 'labourers', 13% were in trade, and another 13% participated in clerical jobs."[27]

A study in Winnipeg, Manitoba, in 1977, however, found that wife batterers were disproportionately represented in three occupations - truckdriver, police officer and doctor.[28]

Interpreting These Profiles

It bears repeating that the above statistics should <u>not</u> be interpreted as statistics on battered wives across Canada. They are statistics on one group of battered wives who went to transition houses for help in 1978. This does not reduce their impact or their validity. Still, they must not be used to conclude that middle and upper-class women are rarely battered.

Middle-Class Wife Battering

Many transition house workers spoke of the web of silence around middle and upper-class wife battering. Their information on middle-class wife battering comes primarily from doctors, lawyers, police and social workers who refer women to their houses, but also from middle-class women who may phone for advice, but don't stay in the house. Transition house workers reported that middle and upper-class women frequently believe that wife battering is a "lower-class" phenomenon and won't admit that it has infested their homes. They may also seek medical attention or look for legal solutions more readily than lower-income women and because these outside channels do not keep figures on wife abuse these women become invisible victims.

A few reports and statistics, however, confirm our conviction that wife battering is just as common in middle and upper-class homes.

[23] Ibid., p. 6.

[24] Gayford, J.J., "Battered Wives" in Martin, J.P., op. cit., p. 21.

[25] Ibid., p. 27.

[26] Quoted in Goldman, op. cit., p. 49.

[27] Chan, op. cit., p. 7.

[28] Study done by Osborne House workers, Winnipeg, Manitoba, 1977.

The proportion of domestic homicides is most markedly above average among suspects in the two white-collar occupational categories of "professional/managerial" and "clerical/commercial".[29]

[29] Statistics Canada, op. cit., p. 100.

Sidney Katz in a Toronto Daily Star article "Battered Wives Seek Refuge" found that "police and social workers will tell you that some of the most inveterate wifebeaters are lawyers, doctors and business executives".[30]

[30] Davidson, Terry, Conjugal Crime: Understanding and Changing the Wife Beating Pattern, Hawthorn Books, Inc., N.Y., 1970, p. 7.

Pollster Louis Harris...found 5% more college-educated people approved of slapping their wives "on appropriate occasions" than the national average did. He concluded that, if anything, the middle class is more prone toward physical assault than the poor.[31]

[31] Ibid., p. 6.

A recent survey in the U.S. found that 23% of middle-class wives charged physical abuse as a reason for seeking divorce.[32]

[32] Ibid., p. 6.

Unfortunately, we do not have Canadian divorce statistics disaggregated by class membership of the applicants, but in general, formal divorces have in the past been more common among the middle and upper classes and so we can assume that these classes have a high representation in the divorce figures, which reveal that at least 1/4 of all divorce applications made in 1978 included physical cruelty in the statement of grounds.[33]

[33] Estimated from figures provided by the Central Divorce Registry, Ottawa, November, 1979.

A Western Michigan University study estimated that wife assault occurs in more than 10 percent of Kalamazoo County's 47,000 families. John Flynn, the director of the study, said although the families they studied came from all social levels, "more than half have a middle or high level of income, education and employment".[34]

[34] Zintl, Terry, Wife Abuse: Our Almost-Hidden Social Problem, Detroit Free Press, January 25, 1976.

Family Services in Thunder Bay, Ontario, an agency used mainly by middle-class clients who pay a fee, found that 19.2% of their clients experienced wife assault.[35]

[35] Support Services for Assaulted Women, op. cit.

Terry Davidson found that battered wives from working-class families in the U.S. seemed to have much stronger resources than middle-class wives. Working-class women "seemed to have less fear and more control over their own lives than the middle-class women with whom I spoke. The middle-class wife has more to lose, in status, possessions, and ego-loss. This woman is shattered by the shock of 'lower-class type' behavior appearing in her marriage. There is such a taboo in her world against taking a husband to court or calling the police because of him or even admitting the barbarisms that she has fewer options for relief. And she's aghast at the thought of going on welfare."[36]

[36] Davidson, op. cit., p. 69.

Even a Parliamentary debate in England as long ago as 1860 pointed out that "If the revelations of the Divorce Court" were any guide, "brutal assaults were by no means confined to women of the lower classes."... "Since few ventured to study divorce cases and most information was derived from police records, conjugal violence was assumed to be a lower-class trait."[37]

[37] May, Margaret, "Violence in the Family: an Historical Perspective" in Martin, J.P., op. cit., p. 144.

Finally, we will let middle-class women speak for themselves:

Most of us don't want to break up our homes if finances are not our problem.

There is such a stigma attached to this problem especially in the middle and upper-class that the real need seems to be somewhere to get advice and counselling without a lot of red tape and publicity. Calling the police is often out of the question.

Why should a woman become poverty-stricken, without the house she has tended for many years, with her lifestyle drastically altered because a husband or other man has abused her?

I put up with not only physical abuse, but all kinds of mental abuse also because I had six children to care for. The men who abuse their wives are in a class by themselves. Only the women know the real story. These men seem to think that the women have no rights and the government supports this view when they don't make the men pay support to the wives when they leave. Today I am old before my time. I am living on $300.00 a month while I work my way through college, supporting my daughter. My husband earns $22,000.00 a year. That is my payment for 22 years of marriage![38]

[38] Quotes again taken from *Women in Transition, op. cit.*

How Much Wife Battering Is There in Canada?

There has been no national survey in Canada to determine the incidence of unreported or untreated cases of wife abuse. Even many reported cases of wife battering are not captured statistically because police, hospital and social service statistics do not systematically differentiate wife battering from other forms of assault, accidents, or family problems. As a result no <u>definitive</u> statement about the incidence of wife abuse can be made.

However, the incidence of wife battering can be <u>estimated</u> by first combining known statistics on the number of women who are in transition houses because they are battered with the number of women who file for divorce on grounds of physical cruelty. Then these figures can be adjusted to represent total numbers since houses are not located in all provinces or regions. Finally, the sum of these totals can be expressed as a proportion of the married female population. This estimate will give a rough indication of incidence, but an indication which is given credibility both by more in-depth studies of incidence in individual Canadian towns and cities, and by recent U.S. household surveys on the incidence and characteristics of wife battering. The figures suggest we are dealing presently with only the tip of the iceberg.

<u>Transition House Statistics</u>

In 1978 a total of 9,688 women stayed in the 47 transition houses or hostels across Canada which sent us statistical reports. Since there are 71 transition houses and hostels which accept battered women across Canada, we can estimate therefore that about 15,000 women would stay in 71 transition houses annually.

Not all of these women were physically battered, however. Many houses, particularly in small towns and rural or isolated areas, which accept women who have been battered also accept women who "just have to leave", or have nowhere else to go, and a few accept women with alcohol problems. A conservative estimate of the proportion of these women who are <u>physically</u> battered when they arrive at a transition house is about 60%. Therefore we know that at least 5,800 women in 1978 went to 47 transition houses expressly because they were physically battered.

However, this is only the number that went to 2/3 of the houses presently existing in Canada. If we add another third to our figure to again approximate the number of battered women who stayed at one of the 71 houses across Canada that we interviewed, our total rises to about 9,000.

In addition, transition houses which kept statistics on the number of women they turned away, report that on the average they cannot accommodate one-third again as many women as they accept. If we add one-third of the total women on top of our figure therefore,

We can estimate that 12,000 women requested help from transition houses because they were physically battered by their husbands.

Now, of course we must remember that the 71 houses interviewed which are currently in operation do not represent all geographic areas in Canada. They tend to be concentrated in large metropolitan centres in the south of Canada and the numbers of houses in the Maritimes, Prairies, Northwest Territories and Yukon are very low. A very generous estimate - not considering such problems as how accessible inner-city houses actually are for women who live on the out-skirts of large metropolitan areas or how many women actually know about the houses even in areas where they exist or how adequate the numbers of houses and their capacities are for the population served - but simply adding the total populations (calculated from the 1976 Census) of the cities, towns and villages that do have at least one transition house, we find that 45% of the Canadian population do not live in areas served by a transition house or a hostel which accepts women who are battered (see Table I). Even if we allow for the fact that there may be more hostels in existence which accept battered women and if we allow for the fact that the populations of individual cities or towns not served could have diminished in some cases, we can safely conclude that:

About half the female population does not have ready access to a transition house or a hostel which accepts women who are battered.

Since we have no reason to assume that there would be fewer battered women who would seek help from transition houses (if they existed) in the areas that are presently not served by transition houses, we can double our figures and conclude that:

If transition houses existed across Canada, we can estimate that at least 24,000 Canadian women would request help from them because they were battered by their husbands.

This estimate does not represent the total number of women who are battered in Canada, but merely a very conservative estimate of the number who would go to transition houses for help if they were available across Canada. As our statistics which detail the characteristics of transition house residents show, middle-class women and women over 35 are under-represented in the transition house population for the reasons we have previously discussed. Divorce statistics give the only existing national data on the possible number of additional women who seek help because they are battered.

TABLE I
1976 Population of Census Metropolitan Areas
Census Agglomeration and Municipalities in Which at Least One Transition House/Hostel was Located as of January 1980.*
(Total population rather than female population was used because sex breakdown was not available for each centre.)

Province	Total Provincial Population	CMA, CA or Municipality In Which Transition Houses are Located[1]	1976 Population of CMA, CA or Municipality	No. of Transition Houses/Hostels Which Accept Battered Women	Provincial Population with No Access to Transition Houses or Hostels
NEWFOUNDLAND	557,725	—	—	—	557,725 - 100%
PRINCE EDWARD ISLAND	118,229	—	—	—	118,229 - 100%
NOVA SCOTIA	828,571	Halifax (CMA)	267,991	1	560,580 - 68%
NEW BRUNSWICK	677,250	Edmundston (CA)[2]	15,851	2	
		Fredericton (Mun)	45,248	1	
			61,099	3	616,151 - 90%
QUEBEC	6,234,445	Alma (Mun)	25,638	1	
		Amos (Mun)	9,213	1	
		Baie Comeau (CA)[3]	26,635	1	
		Chicoutimi (CMA)	128,643	1	
		Hull (CMA)[4]	171,947	3	
		La Baie (Mun)	20,116	1	
		Latuque (Mun)	12,067	1	
		Montréal (CMA)[5]	2,802,485	9	
		Québec (CMA)	542,158	1	
		Sherbrooke (CA)	104,505	1	
		Trois-Rivières (CA)	98,583	1	
		Valleyfield (CA)	35,920	1	
			3,977,910	22	2,256,535 - 36%
ONTARIO	8,264,465	Atikokan (Mun)	5,803	1	
		Carleton Place (Mun)	5,256	1	
		Chatham (Mun)	38,685	1	
		Eganville (Mun)	1,328	1	
		Guelph (CA)	70,388	1	
		Hamilton (CMA)	529,371	2	
		Kenora (CA)	12,519	1	
		Kingston (CA)	90,741	1	
		Kitchener (CMA)[6]	272,158	2	
		London (CMA)	270,383	2	
		Ottawa (CMA)[7]	521,341	2	
		Orillia (Mun)	24,412	1	
		Pembroke (CA)	18,468	1	
		Sarnia (CA)	81,342	1	
		Sault Ste. Marie (CA)	81,992	1	
		Ste. Catherines (CMA)	301,921	1	
		St. Thomas (Mun)	27,206	1	
		Thunder Bay (CMA)	119,253	2	

Province	Population	Centre	Population	No.	
		Toronto (CMA)[8]	2,803,101	4	
		Windsor (CMA)	247,582	1	
		Woodstock (Mun)	26,779	1	
			5,550,029	29	2,714,436 - 33%
MANITOBA	1,621,506	Brandon (Mun)	34,901	1	
		Winnipeg (CMA)	578,217	1	
			613,118	2	1,008,388 - 62%
SASKATCHEWAN	921,323	Regina (CMA)	151,191	2	
		Saskatoon (CMA)	133,750	1	
			284,941	3	636,382 - 69%
ALBERTA	1,838,037	Calgary (CMA)	469,917	1	
		Edmonton (CMA)	554,228	1	
			1,024,145	2	813,892 - 44%
BRITISH COLUMBIA	2,466,608	Vancouver (CMA)[9]	1,166,348	7	
		Vernon (CA)	22,541	1	
		Victoria (CMA)	218,250	1	
			1,407,138	9	1,059,470 - 43%
NORTHWEST TERRITORIES	42,609		—	—	42,609 - 100%
YUKON	21,836		—	—	21,836 - 100%
NATIONAL TOTALS:	22,992,604			71	10,406,233 - 45%

[1] See definitions at end of table
[2] Includes St-Basile.
[3] Includes Hauterive.
[4] Includes Touraine and Aylmer. The population is derived from the CMA for Ottawa-Hull divided by province.
[5] Includes Longueuil and Ste-Thérèse.
[6] Includes Cambridge.
[7] From Ottawa-Hull CMA divided by province.
[8] Includes Etobicoke.
[9] Includes Burnaby, Langley, Port Coquitlam and Surrey.

SOURCE:

Statistics Canada, 1976 Census of Canada, Volume 1, Population: Geographic Distributions, Municipalities, Census Metropolitan Areas and Census Agglomerations, Cat. No. 92-806 (Bulletin 1.7), Minister of Supply and Services Canada, October 1977.

DEFINITIONS:

Census Metropolitan Area (CMA): The main labour market area of an urbanized core (or continuous built-up area) having 100,000 or more population. CMAs are created by Statistics Canada and are usually known by the name of their largest city. They contain whole municipalities (or census subdivisions). CMAs are comprised of (1) municipalities completely or partly inside the urbanized core, and (2) other municipalities, if (a) at least 40% of the employed labour force living in the municipality works in the urbanized core, or (b) at least 25% of the employed labour force working in the municipality lives in the urbanized core.

Census Agglomeration (CA): A geostatistical area created by Statistics Canada comprised of at least two adjacent municipal entities. These entities must be at least partly urban and belong to an urbanized core having a population of 2,000 or more. The urbanized core includes a largest city and remainder, each of which has a population of 1,000 or more, and has a population density of at least 1,000 per square mile (386 per square kilometre). CAs with an urbanized core of 100,000 or more (based on previous census figures) are called census metropolitan areas.

Municipality (Mun): Area with corporate status governed by Provincial and Territorial Acts. These acts differ from province to province. Moreover, municipalities within each province vary in name, status and administrative powers.

(Definitions quoted from Statistics Canada Cat. No. 92-806.)

* Population totals for CMAs, CAs and Municipalities were used rather than population totals for individual centres to estimate the number of people with any access to transition houses. When a municipality within a CMA or CA has a transition house within its limits, it is noted.

19

Divorce Statistics

National divorce statistics provide startling figures.

Almost 20,000 divorce applications in 1978 included physical cruelty in their grounds.

In 1978 there were 71,714 applications for divorce; 47,522 of these were requested by women. A total of 2,800 were applied for on grounds of mental or physical cruelty only. These figures are not particularly shocking, but if we now look at all divorce applications based on multiple grounds, out of a total of 21,654, 17,116 include physical cruelty.[39] Adultery, in contrast, was only included in 7,847 multiple grounds applications.[40]

Certainly some of the applications for divorce on grounds of physical cruelty are by men - no sex breakdown was available. In addition, there is no doubt some overlap between women who stayed in transition houses and those who applied for divorce. Even taking these possibilities into account, however, combining our divorce statistics with transition house statistics we can be certain that at least:

40,000 - 50,000 women in Canada in 1978 suffered sufficient physical and mental abuse to seek outside help.

There are about 5 million couples in Canada. This means that approximately:

One out of every hundred women in Canada married or living in a common-law relationship is battered and has filed for a divorce on grounds of physical cruelty or has approached a transition house for help (given the extrapolation discussed above).

Miscellaneous Canadian Sources

There are other indications that the actual incidence is much higher. A more accurate count would have to include many other statistical sources. For example, we have included no statistics for women who went to social service agencies for help, no statistics for women who went to hospitals and, most importantly, no statistics for the number of calls which police receive regarding family disputes. We did not include these because they are not available nationally. A few local studies are included to give some idea of the cases we missed.

In July 1976, caseworkers in four offices of the Family Services of Greater Vancouver reported 428 cases of wife abuse on their caseloads for this single month.[41] This would represent more than 5,000 annually, because the caseworkers stated that their caseloads fall off in the summer.

In Newfoundland, with a total married female population of 113,855, 834 domestic disturbance calls were made to the Newfoundland Constabulary in 1978; and a family lawyer estimated that he personally had seen between 130 and 200 women who had been threatened or battered in the past year.[42] In addition, 44 charges of assault, 312 charges of bodily fear and 62 charges of drunk and disorderly conduct were brought before St. John's Family Court, which deals only with domestic situations.

A survey of social, medical and legal services in Thunder Bay, Ontario, found that in a city of about 119,000 the number of assaulted women who sought help in one year was 902. [43]

[39] 19,785 divorce applications based on multiple grounds included mental cruelty, but because of the ambiguity of this term, this number was not included in our calculations of incidence.

[40] Provided verbally by the Central Divorce Registry, Ottawa, November, 1979.

[41] Dwyer, Vincent T., "Interspousal Violence: A Response", presented at the second International Conference on Family Law, Montreal, June 13-17, 1977.

[42] The Newfoundland Status of Women Council collected these statistics through a summer student project conducted under the sponsorship of NSWC and the Newfoundland Association of Social Workers.

[43] Support Services for Assaulted Women, op. cit.

20

[44] MacLeod, Flora, ed., *Family Violence: Report of the Task Force on Family Violence*, United Way of the Lower Mainland, Vancouver, B.C. May 1979, Appendix 4, p. 2

[45] Levens, Bruce, & Dutton, Donald, "Domestic Crisis Intervention: Citizens' Request for Service and the Vancouver Police Department's Response", *Canadian Police College Journal*, Summer 1977, p. 40.

[46] Telephone conversation with an officer from the Ontario Provincial Police, October, 1979.

[47] De Koninck, Maria, *Réflexion sur la condition des femmes violentées*, Conseil du statut de la femme, Quebec, 1977, p. 9.

[48] Handleman, Mark, & Ward, Wendy, *Battered Women: Emergency Shelter and the Law*, University of Windsor, 1976, p. 8.

[49] Strauss, Murray, *Behind Closed Doors: Violence in the American Family*, Doubleday, N.Y. (to be released in 1980). Figures reported in the *Calgary Herald*, October 2, 1979.

Between 4,000 and 5,000 women are beaten to the point of serious injury each year in the Lower Mainland (of British Columbia) alone. [44]

Vancouver police receive on average 44 domestic violence calls daily on Friday, Saturday and Sunday and 38 calls daily every other day.[45] That's a total of about 14,768 calls a year.

In 1978 the Ontario Provincial Police investigated 8,340 reported cases of violence and 6,839 - many of them family violence cases - were found to be true cases of assault.[46]

In Baie Comeau, a town with a population of less than 30,000 inhabitants, 4 to 5 domestic violence calls are received daily by a telephone crisis line - that's about 1500 calls a year.[47]

The above figures suggest that the number of calls the police receive is far above the number of cases of women who go to transition houses or file for divorce because they are physically battered. And other studies indicate that even calls to police by battered wives reveal only a glimpse at the magnitude of the problem. For example, a University of Windsor study in 1976 estimated that:

There are ten unreported cases for every call by a battered wife to the police.[48]

If we accept this approximation that there are ten hidden cases of wife battering for every known case, and then apply this proportion to our previous calculation that one in every one hundred women will approach a transition house or apply for a divorce because she is battered, we can estimate that;

Every year, 1 in 10 Canadian women who are married or in a relationship with a live-in lover are battered.

U.S. studies of incidence based on household surveys suggest that this estimate is probably conservative. For example, Strauss, after his recent interviews with more than 2,000 families across the United States, estimated that 16 out of every 100 couples in the U.S. had experienced one or more violent incidents.[49] Therefore, although the above statistics are not all strictly comparable and do not lead us to a firm figure on incidence, they nevertheless support our conclusion that domestic violence is a much more widespread phenomenon than is generally believed.

CHAPTER III

COMMON BELIEFS ABOUT THE CAUSE OF WIFE BATTERING

Any phenomenon which brings harm and even death to a large proportion of the population creates widespread public concern and speculation about its cause in the search for its eradication. Wife battering is no exception. Many theories have been put forward and "cures" tried, and yet the incidence of wife battering has not appeared to diminish, and women who have been battered are asking for different approaches. The most prominent causal theories will be summarized below, with a commentary on why they may be ineffective or inappropriate.

The comments all highlight the conclusion that wife battering cannot be seen as a personal problem which can be treated on an individual level, nor can it be treated as a static phenomenon which can be "explained" with one cause or even a concrete set of causes. Any search for cause assumes that the phenomenon and the cause can in some way be separated from our daily lives, plucked out once the cause is found, and eradicated. But what if the problem permeates the fabric of our lives? Wife battering is so deeply rooted in our society that the treatment itself frequently perpetuates the problem. The treatment, and the beliefs about the causes of wife battering which are behind these treatments must also be recognized as part of the problem of wife battering - part of the psychological battering women experience when they ask for help to stop the battering. As much as possible, the commentaries on these theories and treatment approaches will reflect knowledge and opinions expressed by women who have been battered, or researchers who have interviewed women who are victims of wife abuse.

Alcohol

Statement of Theory: According to this school of thought, alcohol is involved in almost all cases of wife abuse. It is said to be a causal agent which may abnormally alter the personality of the drinker and cause him/her to perform actions which would ordinarily be out of character and against his/her will.

Commentary: Alcohol is in fact present in a large number of cases of wife abuse. But although early studies place the use of alcohol by the aggressor at 80 - 90%, more recent studies show that in less than one-third of the disputes had one or both of the disputants been drinking.[50] Our statistics place the incidence slightly higher - at about 50% for the men and 20% for the women.

Use of alcohol, however, does not make it a causal factor although it may be a facilitator. Many have argued that the fact that we believe alcohol leads to "out of character" behaviour makes it a perfect tool to use to justify violent actions. Gelles argues "When the occurrence of violence in the home becomes public knowledge, or when it is discussed by family members, the deviancy must be accounted for ...Thus individuals who wish to carry out a violent act become intoxicated in order to carry out the violent act."[51]

As one woman reveals,

> He'd come home after work, after being out with another woman the night before and pretend to be drunk even though he'd probably only had a beer or two - just so he could pick a fight.

A project in Kingston, Ontario, also found that violence may be successfully stopped after counselling sessions, even though drinking problems continue.[52] In other words, instead of men beating their wives because they have been drinking,

[50] Levens, Bruce R., "The Social Service Role of Police in Domestic Crisis Intervention", unpublished, 1978 Chan, op. cit., p. 9.

[51] Gelles, op. cit., p 114

[52] Support Services for Assaulted Women, op. cit.

they drink to help justify the fact that they beat their wives.

A Vancouver study gives further insight into this phenomenon:

> *What may be significant (about men going out drinking together*
> *frequently) is the support and encouragement that men give each other in*
> *reaffirming their role as breadwinner and boss. This may partly explain*
> *the fact that women get beaten up more readily after their husbands*
> *return from such drinking gatherings.* [53]

The problem then is not alcohol, it is the social use of alcohol to legitimate violence and to reinforce a certain image of family relationships.

Mental Illness

Statement of Theory: Wife batterers are often characterized by this group of theorists, as typically passive, indecisive and sexually inadequate, while their wives are aggressive, masculine and masochistic.[54] Others with this theoretical orientation claim that wife batterers are frequently psychopathic and all the legislation and punishment in the world will not change their methods of expressing their frustrations.[55]

Commentary: Wife battering is too widespread to be explained primarily by mental illness. Emphasis on this aspect of the problem as the main cause is unlikely to lead to any workable social program since it focuses purely on the individual, not on the whole situation. Unfortunately, studies which provide psychiatric diagnoses for people who are not institutionalized, are rare. However, it is estimated that only 3% of those men who beat their wives have any organic brain damage.[56] Another study shows that irrational attacks which might be described as temporary insanity are very infrequent.[57]

Natural Male Aggression

Statement of Theory: This theoretical leaning has produced two major schools of thought:

1. Male hormones and sexual drives are said to produce violence, especially if the male is deprived of body touch, contact and movement.[58]

2. It is also claimed that the expression of normal aggression between family members releases tension and prevents severe violence.[59]

Commentary: Both of these theories are often used to excuse the attacker and blame the victim for being cold, aloof and insensitive to the attacker's day-to-day needs. However, as one proponent of a modified biological theory reminds us, "Human needs are insatiable because they are in such great part social."[60] That is, we are taught to need at certain times, in certain ways. Other studies show that some violence is not cathartic. Therefore a little violence is not likely to prevent a lot of violence. Modern social psychological theories state:

> *The more frequently an act is performed the greater the likelihood that it*
> *will become a standard part of the behavior repertory of the individual*
> *and of the expectations of others for that individual.* [61]

Finally, if hormones are the true cause of violence, how can violence by the male role model in lesbian relationships be explained? Maleness may be one cause of wife battering, but evidence suggests that it is a socially - learned maleness - a male role - not a biologically determined maleness that precipitates violence.

[53] Epstein, Ng, & Trebble, *The Social Organization of Family Violence: An Ethnography of Immigrant Experience in Vancouver*, Women's Research Centre, Vancouver, 1978, p. 27.

[54] Snell, Rosenwald & Roby's theory of 1964 as reported in Gelles, *op. cit.*, p. 143.

[55] Pizzey, Erin, *Scream Quietly or the Neighbours Will Hear*, Penguin Books, 1974

[56] Youngberg, Iris, *Men as Batterers*, Vernon Transition House, report on workshop at University of British Columbia "Working with Men Who Use Violence", p. 2.

[57] Langley, Robert, & Levy, Richard C., *Wife Beating: The Silent Crisis*, Pocket Books, New York, 1977. Footnote 41, p. 188.

[58] Prescott, James W., "Body Pleasure and the Origins of Violence", in *the Futurist*, April, 1975.

[59] Preface to Steinmetz & Strauss, *op. cit.*

[60] Van Den Berghe, Pierre L., "Bringing Beasts Back In: Toward a Biosocial Theory of Aggression", *American Sociological Review*, Vol. 39, December 1974, p. 778.

[61] Steinmetz & Strauss, *op. cit.*, p. 14.

The Wife Was to Blame

Statement of Theory: According to this popular theory, the victim of intra-family violence is said to verbally torment the aggressor mercilessly, usually by nagging, arguing over drinking and gambling and criticizing sexual performance, until the aggressor is deprived of self-control and reacts violently towards his tormentor.[62]

[62] Schultz, as discussed on p. 55 of Goldman, op. cit.

Commentary: This position is a close relative of the biological theory. It blames the victim and attributes wife battering to temporary insanity. It also tends to focus all attention on individual couples and their particular modes of interaction. When, according to our estimates, at least one in ten couples in Canada are experiencing "interaction aberrations," it seems necessary to look beyond the individuals.

Also, the stereotyped image of the nagging wife has been challenged by other researchers. "In Dr. Gayford's study of British battered wives, 77% of those interviewed reported that physical assaults were usually not preceded by verbal arguments."[63] "Wolfgang found that, of those victim-precipitated killings that involved spouses, significantly more husbands were victims than wives."[64]

[63] Goldman, op. cit. p. 58.

[64] Ibid., p. 60-61.

Reports by women about their husbands' view of the "cause" of the battering also put this "victim precipitation" theory in serious question:

> I myself was beaten by a man I was only living with when I came home later than him one evening. I had stopped to visit friends for a couple of hours. He of course thought I was out with another man! He struck me so hard in the eye that I was blinded for one day. I was afraid of losing my sight in that eye permanently. Of course, it was O.K. for him to see and even sleep with other women…he would even bring them home after I was in bed and 'entertain' them in the living room.[65]

[65] Women in Transition, op. cit.

[66] Ibid.

> He threw the pot at me because he didn't like the supper.[66]

[67] Ibid.

> My mother was beaten weekly because the number one cause was she had delivered three daughters and cheated him from fathering a son.[67]

These first hand accounts put the credibility of any theory which sees violence as the natural culmination of intolerable patterns of interaction, in serious question.

Violence Is Passed on from One Generation to the Next

Statement of Theory: The Proposal put forth in this theory is that violent individuals and battered wives grew up in violent families where they witnessed violence or were victims of violence as children. Therefore the child is socialized to accept violence as normal, appropriate or inevitable behavior in a marriage.

Commentary: There is much support for this theory. Our study of transition houses and their residents revealed that 36% of the women had been beaten as children as had 56% of their mates. Violence in many forms seems to be a way of life in some families. Silver, Dublin and Laurie in a three-generational study found that "many abusives were simultaneously engaged in spouse beating and their children were rapidly accumulating criminal records for committing physically violent acts."[68] Evidence derived from a large national survey in the U.S. also supports the theory that the more an individual is exposed to violence both as an observer and a victim during childhood, the more likely the individual is to be violent as an adult.[69]

[68] Steinmetz. op. cit, p. 7.

[69] Ibid. p. 105.

Childhood socialization certainly seems to affect adult use of violence. It does not explain all cases of violence, however. Middle-class women who are beaten speak of their reluctance to bring their problems to their parents because "My parents don't even know such things exist". The danger of relying on this causal theory is that it allows people who did not have a violent childhood to distance themselves from the incidence and issues surrounding wife battering, and to explain away their own experiences with wife battering in terms like "I just went crazy one night - It'll never happen again" or "He didn't really beat me - he just slapped me around a little. I got my black eye from falling when I lost my balance." Children who learn to accept family violence as a part of life and to see violence by men against women as legitimate are of course more likely to normalize violence in their own families. Direct childhood experience with violence should be seen, however, as only one way children are taught to accept wife battering. Our lessons about the acceptability of violence run deep and have many channels. A detailed discussion of these lessons will follow in the next chapter.

Status Imbalance

Statement of Theory: Wife battering for these theorists is said to be caused by the liberation of women, and by the woman having a higher education or a better job or earning more money than her husband. A man beats his wife to establish his rightful place as head of the family.[70] (Interestingly, this theory was also popular in the 1830's and 1840's to argue against allowing women and children to work in factories.[71])

Commentary: This theory is based on a model of the family which condones and supports inequality. It is a method used by men who beat their wives to explain their actions. As one study states, "Many of the men resent their wives going out to work even though they know there is no other way."[72] Another study proposes that if the wife questions the husband's authority, violence will result.[73] This theory supports a return to a society and mythical family form which is for most families today impossible. It also begs the question of why many of the women who are battered work in the home in a traditional wife and mother role. Again, rather than accepting this as a causal theory, it is more fruitful to see it as another means of legitimating violence. It also suggests that violence is rooted in unrealistic expectations about the form a family should take.

Alienation and the Inability to Communicate

Statement of Theory: Violent men, according to the alienation theories, experience higher feelings of hopelessness and interpersonal incompetence or just plain boredom, are unable to communicate these feelings to their wives and strike out irrationally to relieve their frustration:

> The bored person who cannot experience anything positive has, however, one possibility to experience intensity, and that is destruction. When he destroys life, then he experiences a sensation of dominance over life, he avenges himself on it because he was not successful in fulfilling this life with meaning. When he avenges and destroys, he proves to himself that life has not been able to cheat him.[74]

Other theorists add the element of communication blocks. "Probably the single most frequently mentioned complaint relating to marital interaction was that one spouse would not discuss the problem."[75]

[70] Presented in Gelles, op. cit., p. 122.

[71] May, Margaret, "Violence in the Family: an Historical Perspective" in Martin, J.P., op. cit., p. 143.

[72] Steinmetz, op. cit., p. 123.

[73] Epstein, Ng, & Trebble, op. cit., p. 27.

[74] Fromm, quoted and paraphrased in Chan, op. cit., p. 266. Seligman & May propose variations on this theory.

[75] Steinmetz, op. cit., p. 122.

Commentary: This theory again tends to excuse the aggressor by letting him hide behind a brooding Marlon Brando image. It individualizes the problem and offers no explanation about why boredom and alienation exist in so many families, or why boredom and alienation express themselves as physical aggression against the wife. This becomes a classic example of treating the symptoms rather than the disease and mistaking the symptoms for the cause.

Stress / Social Pathology

Statement of Theory: This school of thought is based on the premise that we live in particularly stressful times. The claim is made that when a man can't cope with external pressures and society's expectations of him, he eventually breaks and violence is a frequent result. Wife battering is therefore said to be more likely in the lower classes where unemployment, poverty and low-level, routine jobs place more stress on men.[76]

[76] Gelles, Steinmetz, Langley and Levy all present this theory or variations on it.

Commentary: This theory is the only theory of all those we have discussed which looks for cause in the wider society, rather than in the individual or the particular family. It takes a very ethnocentric or culture-bound view, however. Wife battering is far from being a modern phenomenon. It is rooted in our laws, religions and traditions, and reports of violence are found in almost every culture and every historical period for which written documentation exists. Further, although our statistics aren't conclusive, many reports, as we have documented, confirm our position that wife battering is not primarily a lower-class phenomenon, it is simply more visible in the lower classes. Stress cannot be seen as a root cause, although it probably is a facilitator, like alienation, alcohol and status imbalance.

The theories discussed on the previous pages, all deal with the symptoms of wife battering while claiming to deal with the causes. None of these theories answer the two most central questions about wife battering:

Why does so much violence take place in the family?

Why is violence so often directed at the wife?

To answer these questions, and to suggest positive action to diminish the incidence of wife battering, two initial steps must be taken. First, the family must be re-examined - not in terms of particular husbands, wives, children and relatives, but as an institution embodying traditions, beliefs, expectations and roles that perpetuate and sanction violence against women in the family. Second, the family as an institution must be explored in the context of other institutions - including legal and medical institutions, with their traditions and roles which reinforce the social acceptance of wife battering in the privacy of the marital home.

CHAPTER IV

ANOTHER LOOK AT THE FAMILY

An Historical View

Wife beating has been condoned throughout history. The first known written laws, thought to date from about 2500 B.C., proclaimed that the name of any woman who verbally abused her husband was to be engraved on a brick which was then to be used to bash out her teeth.[77] Wife beating and wife killing were recognized rights of men in Greek and Roman societies. "Valerius Maximus relates the case of a husband who beat his wife to death because she had drunk some wine" and reports that "his murder, far from being denounced, was not even blamed."[78] Witchhunts in Europe during the Middle Ages included burning women at the stake for scolding, nagging, miscarrying, or talking back to their husbands. "Women in the final stages of pregnancy were burned alive, the heat often bursting their bellies and propelling the fetus outward beyond the fire. The infant was then picked up and flung back into the fire at its mother's feet."[79] Throughout the Middle Ages, wife beating was openly encouraged in the Christian, Jewish and Muslim religions and in countries across Europe. Husbands could kill their wives for adultery without fear of punishment, and wives were expected to give absolute obedience to their husbands. The Renaissance brought no relief to women. It was still believed that a "woman good or bad needs the stick."

The eighteenth and nineteenth centuries also spawned laws that proclaimed man's right to abuse his wife. Napoleon, for example, believed that women must be treated as "lifelong, irresponsible minors," and "legislated women into a position where they were victims of whatever abuse their husbands meted out and wrote no law to protect them."[80] If a woman was beaten by her husband, she had no option but to continue living with him unless her husband also wanted a divorce or she could prove he tried to kill her, which was virtually impossible. British law textbooks in the 19th century still stated that "the husband had by law 'power and dominion over his wife' and could 'beat her, but not in a cruel or violent manner'."[81]

Four themes run through all the historical accounts:

1. that men were considered to own their wives;
2. that, conversely, women were expected to obey their husbands and to conform to the ideal of self-denial;
3. that men had complete authority over their wives that was unquestioned within their own homes;
4. that the woman's place was in the home.

These themes have formed beliefs about what is proper behaviour within the family for centuries. These beliefs have infiltrated laws, religions and modern attitudes and practices, and are still adhered to in varying degrees by the majority of people in our society.

The strong link between these traditions and the prevalence of wife beating is forcefully displayed when we look at periods in history when wife beating was not condoned, and when we examine arguments against proposed reforms to laws which permit wife beating.

For example, in Rome during the Punic Wars, while the men were fighting, the women managed the city. They refused to give up their

[77] Metzger, Mary. "A Social History of Battered Women" p. 59. Copies distributed at consultation for Feminist Services Training Programme Coordinators, sponsored by Secretary of State Women's Programme, Nov. 28-30, 1979.

[78] Ibid., p. 60.

[79] Ibid., p. 61.

[80] Davidson, Terry. Conjugal Crime: Understanding and Changing the Wife Beating Pattern, Hawthorn Books, New York, 1978. p. 104.

[81] May, Margaret. "Violence in the Family: an Historical Perspective," in Martin, J.P., op. cit., p. 139.

positions when the men returned, and as a result they achieved newfound status and wealth. With women now a potential economic asset, fathers did not want large dowries to become the husband's property and so marriages were performed which did not pass ownership of the wife to the husband. Women, at least in the middle and upper classes, thereby gained economic power and independence. As a result they were granted a greater amount of freedom over their persons and their property. Divorce initiated by women became more common and wife beating diminished.[82]

[82] Metzger, Mary. op. cit.

Similarly before the Revolution in France, married women had enjoyed wide freedom and separate property rights, and at least public approval of wife battering diminished.[83]

[83] Davidson, Terry. op. cit., p. 104.

John Stuart Mill's attempts in the 1850's and 1860's to champion the rights of battered women were attacked with arguments which reminded Mill that the place of women was in the home and that if they were encouraged to leave the home, the economy of Britain would be endangered with the increase of "underpaid, superfluous women" in the labour market.[84] In other words, they were saying that policies which increase the economic dependence of a woman and her husband's authority over her may indeed increase wife battering, but these policies should not be questioned since they also protect the economy and preserve jobs for men.

[84] May, Margaret. "Violence in the Family, an Historical Perspective", in Martin, J.P., op. cit., p. 147

This brief historical overview reminds us that the roots of wife battering are nourished by: the acceptance of the husband's total authority in the family, the belief that the wife's proper place is to obey and serve her husband, to be hardworking and all enduring, the resulting immunity of the family to the rules and laws which apply to the wider society and the general societal condoning of wife battering within the privacy of the family home. Placing wife battering in an historical context also alerts us to the fact that the incidence of wife battering is affected by the wife's economic dependence and that wife battering can be used to reinforce the woman's economic dependence.

The Women's View

The first-hand reports of many women who have been battered reiterate the importance of the bonds between: wife battering and economic dependence; wife battering and the general social acceptance of the man's authority over his wife, as well as wife battering and the immunity of the family from many of the rules and laws of the wider society. Women said it this way:

1. On the economic dependence of women on men:

    — *I was in a trap I couldn't get out of — having no money*

    — *I doubt there are very many women who have never been abused by a man in their lives. Our very economic dependence on them brings about many of these undesirable living situations.*

    — *I put up with not only physical abuse but all kinds of mental abuse also because I had six children to care for and needed a home and food for them which I couldn't provide myself.*

    — *My husband used to beat me for years. Now we're divorced and he remarried. His new wife who has her own money — she*

*controls the money and the man. There's no wife beating in this
marriage.*

And a second-hand report:

> — *No matter how high the income bracket of her husband, the
> wifebeater's wife seldom has access to money, even if sometimes
> she herself has a job. . .the husband controls the purse strings
> and demands an accounting of any unfamiliar expense.*[85]

[85] Davidson, Terry,
op. cit., p. 57. It is inter-
esting to note that, of
the houses interviewed
for this study, one house
found that almost half the
women asked to report
on family income had
no idea what their family
income was.

2. On the social acceptance of the man's authority over his wife and
the resulting acceptance of violence by a husband against his wife as
normal and legitimate in certain settings, under certain conditions:

> — *the police are apparently very hesitant to intervene in family
> disputes. . . outside the family, a charge of common assault
> would be laid. It almost seems as though women and children
> have no rights under the present laws. Does marriage give men
> the right to beat their wives?*

> — *the accused seems to have many more rights than the victim in
> these cases;*

> — *I heard the policeman say to my husband - 'Look, I believe a
> man's home is his castle.';*

> — *I couldn't hit him back — it isn't right for a woman to hit her
> husband.*

3. On the immunity of the family from the laws and rules of the
society, and the resulting double isolation of the woman within the family
and within the society:

> — *the worst feeling is that there is nowhere to turn;*

> — *when I lived in this situation there was no one to turn to and I
> put up with it for the sake of the children. The trauma we
> endured at that time was horrible; there was nowhere to go.
> Nowhere to take them, no money to feed them, no alternate
> home to offer them.*

> — *I felt afraid to go outside the house — afraid that people would
> find out, afraid of what they would say — that I was a bad wife
> and deserved it.*[86]

[86] Most of these
quotes are taken from
Women in Transition,
op. cit. Others are
taken from verbal
reports of women's
statements offered by
transition house workers.

An Overview

Wife battering can only be understood by looking at the family not as
a particular and personal group of individuals with all the emotional ties
this image conveys, but as an institution with roles, functions and
traditional relationships with other institutions including law, medicine,
employment and religion. The process of wife battering and the roles the
police, judges, doctors, social workers and others play in its perpetuation
become confused if we concentrate on an individual family with particular
problems and personalities. Wife battering and the network of official
procedures which helps define it is not a personal dilemma, it is an
institutionalized, accepted means of control.

This point requires clarification. Although statistically the Canadian family is changing—there are more single parent families, more people living alone and more families in which two or more people work outside the home than at any time since the depression of the 1930's[87]—many of our institutions are still organized around a model of the family in which there is a strict division of labour and authority based on sex. That is, the man works outside the home and heads the household, while the woman works within the home for her husband, children and other dependent relatives.

[87] MacLeod, Neil, "Incomes of Single Parent and Multi-Earner Families", Staff Working Paper 77-08, Health and Welfare Canada, Ottawa, 1977.

It is clear that many of our institutions have not caught up with the change in family structure when we look at the poverty and loneliness many single parents experience or when we trace the reduction in government-sponsored daycare facilities over the last few years, at a time when more families need daycare either because there is only one parent in the family assuming both parent roles or because both the husband and wife work outside the home. It is also clear that the sex-based division of labour and authority on which the "traditional" family is modelled, is mirrored and so reinforced in the wider society when we observe that most women in the labour force are in low-level positions, earn only about 60% of what men earn, and are concentrated in service and support jobs.[88] To paraphrase Joanie, a character in the Doonesbury comic strip,

[88] Canadian Advisory Council on the Status of Women, Fact Sheet No. 1: Women and Work, Ottawa, 1979.

I do the same work in the daycare center as I do at home—only now I get paid for it!

However, authority by one person over another and differential rewards based on sex are not automatically accepted by women in any society. They must be managed, primarily through socialization. Therefore, women are taught by their parents, relatives, schools, churches and recently the media that it is "natural" and "womanly" for them to accept support jobs, inside and outside the home, that the love and gratitude they will receive for these jobs will make up for the monetary rewards and power they miss. But direct socialization is not always entirely successful and so other safeguards must be built into the society. The most direct safeguard is physical force. However, the society cannot condone physical force in general or anarchy is risked. The solution in Canada and many other societies has been to covertly allow violence as a private matter between husband and wife and so to effectively place the family outside the rules and laws of society. To support this covert system, the "proper roles" for men and women based on a division of labour and authority by sex are built into the rules and procedures of other institutions. Representatives of these institutions learn to turn a blind eye to the use of violence by a husband against his wife in the name of the sanctity of the marriage. The result is that the woman who has been battered looks for help outside her family only to discover that her plea elicits platitudes about the privacy of the home and the proper role of the woman.

Reinterpreting Battering During Pregnancy

The increased likelihood of violence during pregnancy mentioned earlier in this report, provides a striking example to support this argument. The increased dependence and powerlessness of the woman in the family, combined with her isolation from people outside her immediate family during many pregnancies, triggers a response that makes the pregnant woman an appropriate victim—a response that is rooted in our deepest understanding of the role of the family, and the woman's place in it.

While some theorists speculate that battering during pregnancy is really a form of prenatal child abuse—directed at an unwanted child[89]— and others explain this phenomenon in terms of the strain the anticipation of a child places on a relationship and the resulting changes in roles and responsibilities it foreshadows,[90] these explanations don't go far enough.

Both are no doubt important aspects of the situation but should be seen within the context of the wife and family, and the frequent increase in the dependency of the wife on the husband as she often chooses or is forced to quit her job at some stage in her pregnancy. Pregnancy and the birth of children signal for most couples without the financial means to have live-in hired child care, increased rootedness and decreased mobility. Pregnancy also assigns a new care role to the woman in our society—a role which is defined as her "natural" duty, not a role which should properly be assumed by others (witness the continued debates on the negative effects of child care). In addition, pregnancy solidifies the perception of the family as an entity—a unit unto itself. Until the birth of the first child, the outside society is more likely to treat both members of the couple as individuals. After the birth of the first child many women report that people stop treating them as individuals and start seeing them primarily as a representative of the family with a role to care for the children and protect the family unity. This is because pregnancy signals the need for a caretaker for the child and is interpreted as a definitive signal of the "natural" support role of the woman in our society. The husband becomes the individual who represents the entire family outside the home. The birth of a child, in other words, reinforces all our beliefs and traditions which uphold the dependence of the woman and the isolation of the family. But enmeshed with these traditions is the legitimation of violence by the husband against the wife to support her dependency and her isolation. This is not to negate the very real strains and anxiety about new responsibilities which men and women feel before the arrival of a child. It is only to say that wife battering is a common response to these particular stresses because violence, dependence and isolation are intricately meshed in our understanding of the proper role and form of a family.

It is also worth noting that child-rearing is a particularly stressful responsibility in today's society because it signals such intense isolation. Child-rearing is increasingly seen as the total responsibility of the immediate family unit. Child-rearing is not integrated with our other institutions—it is isolated from work and entertainment, among others. So, the highest incidence of wife battering, as our earlier findings showed, occurs during the woman's childbearing years—the years she is potentially the most dependent and the most isolated.

To understand violence in the family, we must look at the way the family is kept isolated, the women dependent and family violence legitimated through family roles, mandates and restrictions and through other institutions in their normal operation. We examined this operational reinforcement of violence by asking why women stay with or return to abusive husbands.

[89] Gelles, Richard J., "Violence and Pregnancy: A Note on the Extent of the Problem and Needed Services", The Family Co-ordinator, January 1975, p. 82.

[90] Ibid.

CHAPTER V

WHY DOES SHE STAY? THE PROCESS OF WIFE BATTERING

Nowhere to Go

About one-third of the women who stay in transition houses return to their husbands. The fact that so many women return to their husbands and many more never leave, has been used as proof positive by those who theorize that women who are beaten deserve it, like it, or are mentally abnormal.

Women stay with husbands who beat them not because they enjoy being beaten, or are psychologically weak, as some of the so-called causal theorists claim: they stay or return because they have nowhere to go. Women who are battered and look for help find there is nowhere to turn for several reasons related to the labour and authority divisions built into our society.

1. First and most important, these women stay because they are isolated. Our society has been organized around the belief that the home is a "haven in a heartless world,"[91] a private and peaceful domain, and that the woman's role in the home is to preserve this privacy and peace. When a woman asks for help because she is being beaten, she challenges this belief and so challenges the very roots of many of our institutions, among them our legal and medical institutions. Our belief that the family is a private part of life that should be immune from prying eyes affects the day-to-day operations of our institutions. It is built right into the rules and regulations which determine how doctors, lawyers, the police, judges and social workers deal with a woman who has been battered and admits to being battered. The result is that the woman frequently is punished by and isolated from the outside world if she ventures into it for help.

Her isolation is reinforced by her day-to-day activities in the family. The woman's role in the home is to preserve for the outside world an image of the family as peaceful and self-contained. Her role is primarily one of helping others, not helping herself. She is used to coping with spontaneous and frequent demands from others, so she has little opportunity and inclination to orient herself to the long-range and detailed plans which leaving her home or eliminating the violence in some other way would demand. She is also constantly faced with the normal daily stress of any family situation and so frequently explains away at least initial bouts of violence as just another normal part of family life. Chan also speaks of this phenomenon:

> I have reported data indicating that the battered women in comparison to non-battered ones are comparatively more inclined to normalize the stressful life events impinging on the family systems, which in turn explains why they have been inactive in seeking help from both social agencies and social and kin networks.[92]

It is important to stress again that the woman who is battered normalizes the violence not because she enjoys it but because it is her role to normalize it. Society expects "a good wife and mother" to keep the family running smoothly and to present a well-ordered, peaceful face to the outside world. The family has been compared by Goffman to a backstage,

[91] Lasch, Christopher, Haven in a Heartless World: The Family Besieged. Basic Books, New York, 1977.

[92] Chan, op. cit., p. 290.

or a dressing room—where wounds and anxieties are soothed, tensions relieved and a professional make-up artist prepares the family members for their parts in the world outside the family.[93] The woman is usually given the job of trainer, psychologist, make-up artist and agent.

As Joy Melville points out:

[93] Goffman, Erving, *Presentation of Self in Everyday Life*, Overlook Press, New York, 1959. Reprinted 1973.

> *Few who have not faced physical assault can understand that immediately afterwards a woman's power of decision-making can completely disappear and she will resort to routine tasks like tidying the drawers or cleaning the stove.*[94]

[94] Melville, Joy, "Women in Refuges", in Martin, J.P., *op. cit.* p. 293.

That is, she resorts to her prescribed role of preserving the image of things as normal in the face of family stress.

Because her work must be largely invisible to perpetuate this image of the family and because her time in the family, whether or not she works outside the home as well, is very demanding, she is isolated from the outside world. This isolation is extreme because it is built on the belief that the family itself should be private—a retreat for family members. The woman within the family is therefore doubly isolated. This isolation discourages her from seeking outside help, and often convinces her that her situation is unique and so that in some ways she has failed as a woman, wife and mother.

2. Secondly, the woman who is battered is frequently economically dependent on her husband. To take purposeful action, real options must be available. Many women who are battered don't have real options. They are economically trapped in their isolation. The statistics presented earlier on women who stayed in transition houses, painted a picture of many women with no recent work experience, little education and little or no money. Even women who come from middle or upper class homes may have no access to money they can control. With no money, she has little hope of finding a place to live, she cannot pay lawyers' fees and so must rely on legal aid and she can't support her children. Economic considerations play a very important part, particularly in the decisions of middle-class women to leave or not to leave a husband who batters them.

> *Many battered wives feel that they must stay in the marriage for the sake of the children.*

It is true that children will have a lower standard of living if their mother leaves. The average wage paid to a woman is only 60% of the average wage paid to a man.[95] Therefore, even if the woman has been in the labour force and possesses marketable skills, her chances of earning what her husband earns are small. Difficulty in finding a job is compounded by the anxiety many women feel in giving out references which could result in their husbands finding them. Nor is alimony or child support necessarily a viable alternative.

[95] Canadian Advisory Council on the Status of Women, *op. cit.*

> *In 1975, the International Women's Year Commission conducted a poll of 1,522 women which revealed that alimony is awarded in only 14% of all cases and that fewer than half of these collect it regularly. Although women are traditionally charged with the responsibility of child-rearing, they are awarded child-support in only 44% of all cases and about 47% of these receive it regularly.*[96]

[96] Goldman, *op. cit.* p. 49.

In many cases, even if the woman receives alimony or support from her ex-husband she will be no better off financially. For instance, if she is receiving welfare, her alimony or support payments will simply be subtracted from her welfare payments, plus she will have the added anxiety of wondering whether his cheques will arrive on time. Some of these women decide that their financial anxieties, plus the continued threat of violence they experience through contact with their husbands about the children, obliterate any advantages they may experience on their own, and so decide to return.

Cutbacks in daycare facilities in Canada have also aggravated the child-care problems a woman faces.

In addition, many women resent the fact that they must leave the house and all their possessions and be forced to live on welfare when they were the victims of assault. Even applying for welfare is difficult.

> *Welfare laws require her to leave the matrimonial home and petition for separation or divorce before she can obtain state aid.*[97]

[97] *Ibid.,* p. 5

Chan's study points out how desperate the woman's economic options really are. Out of 194 women, only three found employment while they were at the house, only 7 were able to place children in daycare and only 5 obtained subsidized apartments in Ontario housing.[98]

[98] Chan, *op. cit.,* p. 10-11.

3. Thirdly, her lack of real options is itself a form of psychological battering which creates fear and indecision. Her fear is frequently fed by threats from her husband that he will take the children or "really hurt her next time". Her indecision, created by her lack of options, is often amplified by her ambivalence about her marriage. Although some men have beaten their wives even before marriage, in other cases the couple may have had many happy years together.

Terry Davidson expresses this dilemma poignantly:

> *For many of these wives, the husband who had once declared his love in courtship had become, with marriage, the woman's closest relative and best friend, the focus of her world. When this same loved one became a Dr. Jekyll-Mr. Hyde, turning from a beloved husband into a wifebeater, the battered wife was thrown into a split situation, where she no longer had her friend to confide in, with no outside world to count on, she had no one to save her from her undreamed-of new enemy. If she were to survive, she had to reorganize her once familiar comfortable life — but with no emotional support at all and with very few inner resources left intact.*[99]

[99] Davidson, *op. cit.* p. 7-8.

Leaving, especially leaving with children, is fraught with very real problems. To make these points clearer, we will examine what happens when a woman who has been battered approaches various professionals, neighbours, family and friends for help. Once again, as much as possible our information will be taken from first-hand reports both from the women who have been beaten and from the transition house workers who may contact or be contacted by other help agencies on behalf of the women or who may accompany women who have been beaten to police stations, courthouses, lawyers' offices, welfare offices and hospitals.

The Medical Response

Doctors are not required to report or question suspected cases of wife abuse. Medical training furthermore is generally concerned with individual pathology and individual cure. Although the recent approach to medicine labelled "holistic medicine" may change the orientation of the medical profession, currently most doctors do not attempt to treat an experience or a situation, they attempt to treat an individual's symptoms. So, one woman who had been beaten throughout her pregnancy went to her doctor (a friend of her husband's) in her eighth month and asked him for help with her problems and her injuries. "The doctor told her coldly he was treating her for prenatal checkups and delivery only; he did not want to know about anything else."[100] Emergency departments, short of time and staff, may treat the woman perfunctorily. Her injuries are taken care of, but nobody asks why she has been a regular visitor to emergency over the past year.

[100] Davidson, op. cit., p. 85.

A statements by a physician clearly expresses the "value-free" approach many doctors take to cases of wife-battering.

> If a woman comes in with bruises, I ask about the cause. If she says, "I fell down the stairs", I accept her explanation. Upon examination, however, I may feel that she didn't sustain these bruises by falling down the stairs. Somebody may have hit her. I accept the patient's story . . . We don't have the time or the background for the reason of the assault. . . It's a personal problem between man and wife.[101]

[101] Davidson, op. cit., p. 84-85.

Probably the most dangerous and isolating result of the medical viewpoint and the treatment options that result is that many doctors characterize wife battering as a psychiatric problem of the woman. She is then either given tranquilizers or referred to a psychiatrist.

> Psychiatric referrals . . . follow non-battering injuries only four percent of the time, while the largely unidentified victims of battering were referred 15% of the time to emergency psychiatric facilities, clinics, local community mental health centers or the state mental hospital. Mental health practitioners tend to place too much emphasis on maintaining the family unit intact as a therapeutic goal.[102]

[102] Response to Violence and Sexual Abuse in the Family - a project of the Center for Women Policy Studies, Vol. 2, No. 7, May-June 1979.

Gayford also found that 46% of women who had been battered and gone to an emergency department had been referred for psychiatric opinions.

> Some women know that they were regarded as having personality disorders and being a nuisance to the psychiatric service . . . Most psychiatrists do not like treating cases where there is an element of marital violence as the case can be very time-consuming and the results poor.[103]

[103] Gayford, J.J., "Battered Wives" in Martin, J.P., op. cit., p. 32.

The Response of Social Agencies

Counselling centers respond in much the same way. Most social workers are trained to respect the sanctity of the family and to encourage reconciliation wherever possible. Helen Levine, a social worker and leader in the feminist counselling movement in Canada, sees the problem from both sides.

> By and large, women have found that helpers stressed adjustment

[104] Levine, Helen. "On the Framework of Women's Lives and Feminist Counselling", Ottawa, 1978.

rather than change; individual, not collective solutions; individual pathology instead of social conditions; weakness rather than strength; the psyche, unrelated to the economic and political conditions of women's lives. [104]

Many social agencies, under the guise of "fairness" and an attempt to see both sides of the story, distribute the blame and the violence evenly. In some cases this may be true, but in almost all cases strength and the severity of the violence is not evenly distributed, and an emphasis on identifying blame or guilt individualizes the problem and does nothing about overcoming it. The counselling approach tends to define the man's actions as a temporary form of irrationality and to therefore absolve him of real blame. But wife battering cannot be seen as a problem of interaction in an individual couple. It is too widespread to accept this explanation. When at least one-tenth of the married population either batters or is battered, the source of wife battering must be located in structural causes.

Women also report that social agencies are frequently geographically inaccessible and are usually open during normal working hours only. As we documented before, most wife battering occurs after normal working hours. The counsellors are therefore not available when the women need them the most.

And most important, counselling doesn't work, according to many women, because it has only short-term effects at best, and because their husbands refuse to be involved.

[105] Women in Transition, op. cit.

The results of our family counselling only lasted six months and then the fists and drinking started again. [105]
He wouldn't go to a counsellor—he said there was nothing wrong with him. What good is marriage counselling with one person?

The reluctance of men who batter their wives to go to a counsellor is well documented by professionals as well. Attempts have been made in the U.S. to introduce counselling programs for men who batter their wives, but these programs constantly run up against the problem that "Most of the time, violent husbands refuse (therapy), insisting there is nothing wrong with (them)." [106]

[106] Langley & Levy, op. cit., p. 22. This point was also made by the Director of Therapy for Abusive Behavior in Baltimore, Maryland.

The Response of Friends and Family

The woman may not even find that she has the emotional support of her friends and family if she admits she is battered. Many battered wives have been systematically isolated by their husbands and by their own shame about their situation and so have no one they feel they can approach. Other women are shocked to find that their friends and even their parents side with the men and tell the women they are exaggerating or must try to be better wives so they won't lose their homes and husbands. One woman told the story about calling her mother after being badly beaten. Her mother reluctantly agreed to take her in. When the husband followed his wife there and beat her again, the mother asked her to leave because "she couldn't stand that much violence". Other women report:

You know you're really alone when you try to stay with friends. Oh, some of them are sympathetic, but no one wants to let you stay in case they'll be in danger.

Some of my family gave me moral support but no money.

Where Else Can She Go?

Transition houses are often the only alternative for a woman who has no money and must get away from her husband. Unfortunately, many areas of the country do not have transition houses, women often don't know about houses in their vicinity and social agencies and police frequently don't refer women to transition houses. The houses that exist are forced to turn away one-third of the women who come to them because of overcrowding and as a result of funding regulations they cannot accept all women—particularly working women or women without children.

The Police Response

The isolation of the family and of the woman within the family is most clearly exemplified in the legal response to the battered woman. The range of legal options available to the woman who has been battered and the inadequacies of these options will be discussed in depth in the following chapter. The present discussion will therefore be limited to the police response with the caveat that police action policies cannot be divorced from the policies of actors at other levels of the legal system. It must also be emphasized that it is not specific individual lawyers, police officers or judges that are being criticized, nor is it doctors, psychiatrists or counsellors as single individuals who were being discussed in the previous section. While individuals must be held accountable for their actions, the problem lies not primarily in the specific individuals whom the "battered wife" encounters in her search for help, any more than it lies in the individual woman who is battered or her batterer. The problem with the medical, social work and legal responses to wife battering lies in the programmed responses, i.e. the training the individuals undergo to fulfill their roles, and the rules, regulations, professional ethics and expectations which create the modes of action carried out by these individuals. The police do not have clear guidelines defining how to deal with a case of wife battering. Because they have unclear guidelines, they frequently choose a common human retreat—they deny that the situation exists or they avoid it as much as possible.

Women's reports of their experiences with legal authorities display this retreat policy:

- *The police refused to interfere.*

- *The detective informed my sister (abuse victim) that he didn't believe the incident occurred.*

- *Police just said to keep the peace.*

- *The police are apparently very hesitant to intervene in family disputes.*

- *The hassle with judges, Justices of the Peace, is almost not worth it. There are dozens of calls to make and people to see before you get any action. There are a lot of women out there who don't know what to do so they return to the same situation.*[107]

[107] *Women in Transition, op. cit.*

108 Chan, op. cit., p. 10.

followed through the larger part of the prosecution process and laid assault charges.[108]

The role of the police is ambiguous. On the one hand they have a duty to uphold the peace, on the other they have a duty to stop crime and protect the victim. In family dispute cases these duties frequently become contradictory. Many men are incensed that the police have been called and become more violent both towards their wives and towards the police officers. Although Canadian figures aren't as high as U.S. figures, still 14.6% of 41 Canadian policemen (killed between 1961 and 1973) were killed while intervening in family disputes.[109] Police know therefore that they face personal danger when they enter a home and they know that if they arrest the man the woman can suffer a retaliatory beating when he gets out of jail. The solution adopted by many departments is first to minimize the number of cases they get involved in —

109 Levens & Dutton, op. cit., p. 31.

> A study of Vancouver police revealed that in 45% of husband/wife disputes where police presence was requested, the police responded in advice only.[110]

110 Levens & Dutton, op. cit., p. 44.

and secondly to accept a non-arrest policy and try to "cool the situation out" instead. This perspective is not entirely without reason. Not only do police know that many families will suffer loss of financial support if the husband is imprisoned and that many men retaliate against their wives when they are released, they also know that if the husband is arrested he will probably be promptly released from custody under the provisions of the Canadian Criminal Code and also that the sentence handed down against him will likely be very lenient.

> A judge will not send a man with a good salary to prison and put his wife on welfare. In terms of our social values, his capacity to earn money is of greater weight than the probability that he will injure his wife.[111]

111 "The Situation of the Battered Woman". New Woman Center Journal. Vol. 1 No. 2, October, 1977.

There are also many cases where, for many of the above reasons, the wife does not want her husband arrested — "she may have called the police in order to have him removed from the premises until his violent outburst passes, to frighten him into good behaviour and/or to use the threat of arrest as a future defence, or perhaps to obtain medical attention.[112]

112 Goldman, op. cit., p. 66.

The police officer's dilemma is therefore between no-enforcement and full-enforcement when he lacks special training, and either choice may trigger a killing.[113] The officer's effectiveness may be further compromised because police are also members of the wider society and so share general beliefs about the privacy and peace of the family and the woman's role within the family. A well publicized case in which a police officer was quoted as saying "If it had been my house, I would have beaten my wife for the condition it was in"[114] brings the point home. Because police officers do frequently share the belief that a man's home is his castle, and because the way they handle the situation is usually left to their discretion, the way they "cool the situation out" is frequently to side with the man and so to reinforce the woman's feelings of isolation and helplessness. Alternatively they may treat the situation in a cold "objective" way that treats the injuries as the deciding factor in policy. One common practice is to arrest the man only when he has inflicted a wound requiring a given

113 Goldman, op. cit., p. 67.

114 Calgary Herald, June 29, 1979.

number of stitches. The woman learns that calling the police is not a solution to her dilemma.

Even if the man is arrested, the "cooling the situation out" policy frequently still applies. Obstacles, primarily in the form of delays, may be placed in the victim's way in order to test her desire for a conviction.[115] For instance, the woman may be told that she may seek a peace bond against her husband even though it is recognized that these peace bonds are not really enforceable. Their enforcement amounts to a legal slap on the wrist and warnings, a peace bond does not remove the man from the house, and so the woman who has been beaten must continue to live with the man who has been beating her.

[115] Goldman, op. cit., p. 68.

What Can the Woman Do? - The Inevitable Cycle

When there is nowhere to turn—no real viable option—she stays in her situation and tries to normalize it to keep her sanity. In other words, the psychological battering she has experienced looking for help reinforces her dependence on her husband. It must be remembered that the situation she is in can literally "drive her crazy", so much of her energy must be spent combatting her psychological battering.

> Mental battering or abuse can cause as much, or more, distress as physical battering, and accounts for a high proportion of women in refuges. Very often it is constant humiliation by the husband—who is set on ridiculing his wife in public, or proving her wrong, to reinforce his own superiority. Insults and constant criticism can reach intolerable heights—whether sexual taunts or accusations about being a bad wife and mother. When it goes on for hour after hour, the woman is confused by it as after physical battering. She loses her confidence in herself and her general ability to cope.[116]

[116] Melville, Joy, "Women in Refuges" in Martin, J.P., op. cit., p. 303.

To cope with the situation she frequently accepts the guilt. This acceptance is easy since it is the option which may have been offered her by counsellors, doctors or policemen. It is also easy to do with her battered self-esteem, and she may have learned, particularly if she came from a family in which violence was an accepted form of expression, that battering is part of the lot of women's lives. Even if this was not the case, women are taught that they hold the major responsibility for the success or failure of a marriage. Her shame at "failing" persuades her to contribute to her own isolation and she no longer tries to talk to family, friends or outside officials. Religious beliefs can strengthen her feeling of guilt and increase her abhorrence of the possibility of divorce. Even her children may reinforce her feelings of being inadequate.

> After five or six, there are often strong indications of (children) losing respect for their mother. Some identify with the aggressor instead of the mother; the dynamics can get very confused. One daughter refused to testify against her father, saying very proudly, "My father can beat anyone."[117]

[117] Davidson, op. cit., p. 119.

Some teenagers respond by treating the mother's suffering as "just part of the daily routine". They depersonalize her and block her from their consciousness and conscience. She couldn't be worth much if she got herself into such a fix, now could she?[117A]

[117A] Ibid., p. 119.

Left with nowhere to go and absolutely no one to turn to, the woman is forced to collude in covering up the crime, and the circle is complete.

It is evident from the above discussion that wife battering does not stop at the family door. Wife battering is condoned and reinforced by the day-to-day decisions, attitudes and policies of most people the wife can approach for help. By taking her problem outside her home, the woman who has been battered usually discovers that she is alone in a world of professionals and friends who systematically deny the reality of her own experience.

CHAPTER VI

WIFE BATTERING AND THE LAW

The weak sentencing and arrest policies which can increase the powerlessness and hopelessness of women who have been battered can only be understood in the context of laws impacting on the family. Laws to protect wives who are battered are in fact technically in place, but accepted legal procedures and exceptions written into the law to protect the unity of the family make convictions virtually impossible and reinforce the wife's isolation and dependence.

A man may no longer have the legal right to beat his wife under the letter of the law, but many legal procedures still support the power of the husband over his wife, and so help encourage the societal acceptance of violence in the family. As Goldman states,

> *The subordinate status ascribed to women and wives in law, and the superior authority granted to men have had no uncertain effect upon the use of force to control women. In his research on divorce-prone families, O'Brien found that men frequently employ physical force against their wives in order to maintain the position of superiority that society expects of them. In so acting, they have been influenced by both law and tradition.*[118]

[118] Goldman, *op. cit.*, p. 17.

It is undeniable that laws have a considerable influence in shaping the values of society as well as reflecting the attitudes of those who framed them. When these values are in question, the law must also be put under scrutiny.

To clarify the discussion of laws and legal procedures surrounding wife battering which follows, the areas of provincial and federal authority with regard to the law in Canada should be reviewed. According to the British North America Act, certain laws are placed within federal jurisdiction—criminal law and divorces for example—while others, including property and family laws, fall within provincial jurisdiction. Laws under federal jurisdiction are administered by the individual provinces, but can only be amended by the federal justice system. Laws under provincial jurisdiction are both administered and amended by the individual provinces. As a result, considerable variation can exist from one province to another in laws under provincial jurisdiction.

Technically, a woman who has been battered has five main legal options. Three of them are under federal jurisdiction. Under the criminal code, she may charge her husband with assault, or apply for a peace bond; and under the Divorce Act she may divorce him on grounds of physical cruelty. Her fourth and fifth options—applying for an injunction or for an ex parte interim order—fall under provincial jurisdiction. Each option will be discussed in turn. No attempt will be made to present an exhaustive critique of the laws surrounding wife battering. Instead some of the more blatant incongruities between the legal treatment of wife battering and other forms of assault will be highlighted, to emphasize how the application of the law indirectly condones wife battering.

The Charge of Assault

A wife who is battered is "the victim of a (federal) criminal offence, whether it be common assault, assault causing bodily harm, or attempted

118A Goldman, *op. cit.*, p. 63, referring to *Criminal Code* R.S.C. 1970, c. C-34, S.244. S.245(2) and S.222.

murder".[118A] Because assault is a criminal offence, it is no longer a crime only between two individuals—it is considered a crime against society.

The Criminal Code includes two different offences under the term "common assault", which is the charge most often laid in cases of wife battering:

1. The use of intended physical force against another person who has not consented to the amount of force that was used;

2. A threat to use physical force or an attempt to use physical force, where the victim has a reasonable fear that the person making the threat was likely to carry it out.

The wife who decides to lay a charge of common assault against her husband can proceed in one of two ways. She can accuse her husband of assault, usually through the police; the crown attorney then decides whether she/he will lay the charge and proceed with the case. Because the police are frequently hesitant to arrest the husband in cases of wife battering, as we discussed in the last chapter, this procedure is usually nipped in the bud. The woman does have another option however, as does any victim in an assault case under the Criminal Code. She can lay a private prosecution. This means that she can personally go to the court office to lay the charge, act as the crown attorney and present the case herself. While this procedure has the advantage of bypassing the police, few women are aware of this right and fewer are given the support and information necessary to present the case convincingly according to the rules of the courts.

119 McKay, Robin. *A Handbook on Domestic Assaults*, commissioned by Kingston Interval House, Box 224, Kingston, Ontario.

The law of assault does technically apply to husbands and wives just as it does to other people, regardless of relationship. Under the law, a wife can take her husband to court on a charge of common assault.[119] However, in reality it is not this simple, first because of police reluctance to arrest, and second because proof of assault in husband-wife cases is almost impossible to provide.

When is Proof not Proof?

Although in most criminal cases the wife can not be forced to testify against her husband according to the doctrine of the unity of spouses, in cases of personal injury this doctrine is waived. However, the evidence she is permitted to give is so constraining that few cases hold up in court.

In almost all wife battering cases, because of prevailing attitudes and tenacious legal prc   ures, a third party who actually witnesses the crime is the only sure proof the woman has to establish her credibility before the court. Since most cases of wife abuse occur in the privacy of the home with no witnesses present, this is frequently impossible. If an eye-witness report does not exist, any report by the wife to a third party—like a police officer, a transition house worker or a neighbour she goes to for help—will only be allowed if the victim was under attack or in immediate and provable danger at the time she made the statement. While the sense of this stipulation is that a woman cannot thereby falsely complain to a neighbour or friend that her husband beat her and then use this false report as evidence to have her husband convicted of assault, the nonsense of this ruling is exemplified by the following case in which a battered woman died of her wounds:

In R. v. Goddard, *neighbours, who had seen the accused husband
enter his home, heard heavy steps pursuing light steps, the sounds
of a struggle and a woman's scream. Although the deceased was
found standing in a pool of blood and was taken to a friend's home
where she identified her husband as her assailant, her declaration
was not held to form part of the* res gestae *(i.e., the permissible
evidence). Only, as in* R. v. Wilkinson, *where her presence in a
neighbour's home could be explained by the fact that she was still
being pursued by her husband, and was aware of the peril, would a
battered woman's declaration be found to form part of the* res
gestae.[120]

[120] Goldman, *op. cit.*,
p. 81-82

Further, if the husband is on trial for assault, he cannot be convicted
on evidence of similar acts of assault in the past, since this is considered
"prejudicial" evidence. Rulings against the use of "prejudicial" evidence are
intended to protect the rights of the accused, and are integral to our justice
system. In cases of wife battering however, they protect the accused, and
can misrepresent the crime as it is experienced by the victim.

*For a battered wife, the criminal justice system may be the last
resort in a series of unsuccessful attempts to terminate the violent
relationship: while the court considers the single assault which is the
subject of the charge, the complainant seeks relief from the ongoing
crime against her.[121]*

[121] *Ibid.,* p. 87.

Finally, a wife who is battered and is legally married to the man who
battered her will often be allowed by the crown attorney to drop the
charges much more readily than would the victim in an assault case
involving strangers or acquaintances, even if the crown attorney knows
that she dropped the charges under pressure from her attacker. The logic
behind this practice is that the woman may change her mind in the light of
day after the heat of the argument has subsided. This logic however
ignores the fact that wife beating is not usually preceded by an argument,
so the woman does not need time to "cool down" and think her decision
over, and that a woman who seeks legal recourse has usually decided she
has no other options. It places the complete burden, not only of the initial
arrest but also of the possibility of conviction, on the woman. Her
husband, knowing that the matter is not out of her hands and irreversible
just because she laid charges, and that the case will be dropped if she
withdraws her complaint, will frequently threaten her with even more
serious future violence against herself or her children, may threaten to
have the children taken away if she doesn't drop the charges, or may
simply once again convince her that her decision was crazy because she
has no real means of financial support without him. Since many women
by the time they get to court have looked for other options and found that
they are virtually non-existent, his words will ring deafeningly true. By
allowing the wife to be persuaded by her husband to withdraw her
complaint, the legal system again is giving official recognition to the
powerlessness of the woman in the home and to the acceptance of wife
battering as a private matter. One woman expresses the confusion and
resignation which results from this legal inconsistency:

I was scared of him — he said he'd get his brother to take the kids away if he ended up in jail and that he'd spend all his time in jail figuring what to do to me when he got out. . . After all he is my husband and they are his children too. . .what else could I do?

The Peace Bond - An Alternative Legal Procedure

The criminal law does provide the woman with another alternative to charging her husband with assault. She may apply for a "peace bond". Peace bonds are applied for through provincial Family Courts, and have one major advantage over assault charges.

In order to get a peace bond, you do not have to prove that a criminal act has been committed, but only that it is likely to occur. [122]

122. McKay, *op. cit.*

The same rulings regarding "prejudicial evidence" and third-party eye-witness proof do not therefore apply. In addition, peace bonds are relatively quick to process. However, the advantages are heavily outweighed by the disadvantages. First and foremost among the disadvantages, a peace bond does not remove the husband from the house unless the couple is already separated. After the woman "lays the information", the husband will be summoned to appear in court on a future date. If in court he admits to the allegations, then he may be ordered to keep the peace and be of good behaviour for a period of not more than twelve months and may be ordered to uphold other reasonable conditions, including for example attending counselling sessions. If the husband does not admit to the allegations, however, then the burden is once more on the wife to provide convincing evidence.

It is generally recognized that peace bonds are not really enforceable. Technically, if the husband disobeys a peace bond, and the wife reports him, he is then in contempt of court, has committed a criminal offence and is liable to a fine and/or a jail term. In reality, however, judges are hesitant to impose stiff penalties because of the financial hardships they can impose on the entire family. Especially if it is a first offence, the charges will probably be dropped. Throughout this entire procedure, unless the couple is legally separated, the woman who has been beaten must cohabit with the man who has been beating her, and the final result is likely to be no more than a legal slap on the wrist and warnings.

Divorce on the Grounds of Physical Cruelty

In Canada, under the federal divorce law, a woman may petition for divorce on the ground that her husband has "treated her with physical or mental cruelty of such a kind as to render intolerable their continued cohabitation". [123] However, "cruelty" as grounds for divorce is unclearly and subjectively defined, leaving the onus again on the petitioner to prove that the violence was "grave, weighty and intolerable" as defined by the particular presiding judge. This means that each case must be weighed on its own merits, in terms of, "for example, the mental and physical condition of the spouses and their position in life, their backgrounds, the society in which they live, and their characters and attitude toward the

123 Goldman, *op. cit.*, p. 104, quoting the *Divorce Act*, R.S.C. 170 C.D.-8. S.3(d).

124 *Ibid.*, p. 107.
marriage".[124] While of course this subjective definition can result in verdicts expressing deep compassion and sensitivity to the woman's plight, because the law indirectly condones the rights of the husband within the home and the sanctity of marriage and because legal training therefore reinforces these values, the verdict is more likely to attempt to uphold the power of the husband and to preserve the marriage at all costs.

The Powerlessness of Injunctions

The woman who is battered has further recourse under provincial legal jurisdiction or civil law. Her first option under provincial law is to apply for an injunction against her husband. Again the barriers against the granting and effective enforcement of injunctions in provinces across Canada compromise the effectiveness of even this tool.

An injunction is a court order prohibiting a husband "from entering the matrimonial home and/or restraining him from molesting or interfering with his wife".[125] Laws regarding injunctions, however, like laws governing assault, were never intended primarily to cover domestic cases. "An injunction can only be granted in support of a legal right."[126] As we have seen in our preceding discussion of the legal rights of wives who are battered, the wife's legal rights are frequently unclear. "The rights of battered wives are complicated by questions of ownership and occupation of the matrimonial home and the duty of wives to cohabit unless relieved of their marital obligations by the court."[127] To be granted an injunction, the woman must not only have the legal right not to be molested, but must also have the legal right to exclude her husband from their home.

125 Goldman, *op. cit.*, p. 115.

126 *Ibid.*, p. 116.

127 *Ibid.*, p. 116

She only has this right if he has abused her and if she accompanies her application for an injunction with an application for divorce or an application under the provincial act for separation.

This stipulation places an unfair onus on the woman. Many women who seek legal aid want immediate effective protection but they do not necessarily want a divorce. To paraphrase the statement of a woman quoted earlier, the last thing most women want to do after the physically and emotionally draining experience of a beating is to immediately face the red tape of divorce proceedings. Most women want their husbands to stop beating them and to be good to them—they don't always consider ending the marriage.

The power of an injunction, even where granted, frequently amounts to little more than a legal scolding. If the husband disobeys the injunction, technically he is in contempt of court, can therefore be tried under the federal criminal law, and so may be fined or imprisoned. (Although possible sentences vary by province, the usual maximum is six months or $500.) But again delays may be involved in establishing sufficient proof that an injunction has been disobeyed, and frequently, especially "if it is a first offence, the judge will use an alternative sentencing provision such as a conditional discharge which places the onus on the husband not to repeat his actions".[128]

28 Ostrowski, *op. cit.*, p. 20-21.

Ex Parte Interim Order

Closely related to the wife's right to apply for an injunction is her right to apply for an ex parte interim order. This is a short-term provincial order which can be granted by a judge either in court or out of court and which can be used to keep the violent spouse out of the home or to order him not to molest his wife. This order is the only legal recourse the woman has which takes force immediately and does not require first finding and serving the husband and giving him notice. It provides very temporary protection since it only applies until the violent spouse can be taken to court on one of the charges or procedures detailed above, or for legal separation or support. This is a tool women can use to get some form of protection when they are in danger, but few police or lawyers inform women of this right. Once again, although the law is in place, the woman's access to the law is limited.

The options open to the battered wife under both federal and provincial laws do not effectively protect her. The delays and the frustrations involved in any attempt both to meet the stipulations for proof and to demand legal rights wear most women down and reinforce their feelings of powerlessness and isolation, for "where a violent husband contests either the civil or criminal actions brought against him, his wife's right not to be beaten will be measured against the competing values of the sanctity of matrimony and the preservation of the family unit".[129]

[129] Goldman, op. cit., p. 164 (emphasis added).

Are Marriages Outside the Law?

Other legal options open to individuals outside marriage but denied spouses within marriage reinforce the conclusion that marriages in many respects are considered outside the law. Two such options are discussed on the following pages.

A Woman Can't Be Raped by Her Husband

The legal definition of rape under the Criminal Code is the act of forcible, fraudulent or otherwise coercive sexual intercourse committed by a male person upon a female person who is not his wife.[130] This ruling once again excuses certain acts within marriage which would not be permitted outside marriage. It is based on the idea that the man and his wife are one under the law and the husband therefore has complete rights over his wife. It is defended on the premise that it would be too difficult to prove lack of consent, and that it would undermine the family unit through unnecessary legal intervention.[131] Once again the woman is isolated and her rights undermined by her membership in the family unit. She has, through marriage, lost the right to outside help.

[130] Criminal Code, R.S.C. 1970 c. C-34, s. 143.

[131] McFadyen, Joanna, "Inter-spousal Rape: The Need for Law Reform", Chapter 9, Eekelaar & Katz, op. cit., p. 194-206.

The removal of the spousal exemption clause in this law is currently under review. If this proposed revision becomes law, it will represent an extremely significant step forward in the recognition of the individual's rights within marriage.

A Woman Can't Sue Her Husband

Civil law is also designed to protect family unity. For example, under civil law in most provinces, a woman cannot sue her husband or a husband his wife, after divorce, for an assault committed during marriage or for injuries received from one or more beatings even if she/he was prevented from earning a living as a result of this assault. (There have been recent reforms in this area. For instance, in Ontario, this exemption has been abrogated under Section 65(3) of the Family Law Reform Act of

Ontario.) This stipulation does not apply to common-law marriages. It should be acknowledged, however, that this legal right even outside marriage is weak.

> *An empirical study conducted at Osgoode Hall Law School in 1966 revealed that only 1.8% of the criminally injured respondents collected anything as a result of tort suits against their assailants.* [132]

[132] Goldman, *op. cit.*, p. 126.

Nevertheless this is yet another outdated law which by denying the wife legal rights against her husband indirectly supports the use of violence against women in the home.

The powerless position of the woman who is battered is emphatically revealed by a judgement laid down in 1975 by a Canadian court.

> *In R. v. Chaisson, a husband who had tied his wife to a chair, taped her mouth, manually abused her and burned her breasts, received a twelve month suspended sentence and an eighteen month probation order. The reasoning of the court was that its primary objective should be to facilitate and not impede the reconciliation of the spouses.* [133]

[133] *Ibid.*, from *R. v. Chaisson* (1975) 11 N.S.R. (2d) 170 (N.S.S.C. App. Div.) p. 97.

In view of this sort of verdict, is it any wonder that a woman would conclude:

> *The accused seems to have more rights than the victim. It's a terrifying experience when you finally get up the nerve to press charges. The hassle with judges, Justice of the Peace, is almost not worth it. There are dozens of calls to make and people to see before you get any action. There are a lot of women out there who don't know what to do, so they return to the same situation.* [134]

[134] *Women in Transition, op. cit.*

What Role Does the Law Play in Wife Battering?

The law both reinforces and helps shape the values Canadians hold about wife battering. These values directly mold the policies developed by police, lawyers and judges to deal with cases of wife battering. They also indirectly influence the treatment women who are battered receive at the hands of doctors, psychologists, social workers and even friends or family. The law therefore significantly limits the options open to women who have been battered, because "although a man no longer has the legal right to beat his wife, the attitudes underlying such behaviour have not been legislated out of existence". [135]

[135] Goldman, *op. cit.*, p. 163.

Two basic principles must be reaffirmed in any attempt to provide more effective legal options for women who have been battered. First, women and men should be given protection against violence whether it occurs within or outside the matrimonial home. Second, our laws should uphold the value that "the use of physical force both within the family and within society is unacceptable behaviour". [136]

[136] *Ibid.*, p. 165.

Presently, the rights of the wife who has been battered often stop at the doorstep of the matrimonial home. Stipulations which separate wife abuse from other forms of assault and rape muddy the role that judges, lawyers and police can play and place the sanctity of the home above the protection of its occupants. Wives must be given the same rights as other citizens to call on the law for assistance and to expect true potential for action, when they feel the law is their only or best possible recourse.

CHAPTER VII

WHAT IS BEING DONE?

The desperate picture painted by the preceding chapters leads to the question: Is anything being done to help women who are beaten by their husbands? Do the actions being taken meet the needs of women who are battered? There are groups in society who are vitally concerned with protecting women who have been battered and reducing the potential for wife beating. They too, however, are frustrated by barriers in the structure of our society, traditions and beliefs which come out in the way jobs are done and rules applied which limit the effectiveness of what they can do.

Transition Houses

The few transition houses in Canada — by providing battered wives with a place to escape their spouses — are perhaps the only sure alternative these women now have. Until the police become more sensitive, until the courts become more sympathetic, and until social services become more available, the only option most of the women have is to flee from their husbands.[137]

[137] Gropper, Arlene & Marvin, Joyce, "Violence Begins At Home", *The Ottawa Citizen*, November 20, 1976.

The first transition houses in Canada intended primarily to house women who are battered were opened in 1972 in British Columbia and Alberta. The next year two more houses opened, in 1974 four more, another 14 between 1975 and 1977 and in 1978 alone 14 houses opened. Unfortunately, the impetus of this trend did not continue. In 1979 only six new houses opened, one more house has just opened this year in Fredericton, and to date according to our information only 12 are in the planning stages to open in 1980.

Hostels which accept crisis victims, among them women who have been battered, have also multiplied in the last decade. Although one such hostel which is still in operation in Montreal opened in 1933, 18 of the 20 other hostels of this type opened during the 1970's.

There are currently 71 transition houses or hostels which accept women who have been battered in Canada. The houses are not evenly distributed across Canada. Two-thirds of the houses are in Ontario and Quebec. There are no houses in Newfoundland or Prince Edward Island (although in P.E.I. women who are battered and need protection are put in motels temporarily), and no houses in the Yukon or Northwest Territories (although two houses are in the planning stages in the north). Most of the houses tend to be located in large urban areas in southern Canada. As a result, rural and northern women are frequently cut off from any access to transition houses.

The birth of a transition house does not mean it will continue to survive. Two of the houses contacted, opened since 1977, were forced to close because of lack of funds. Even though the highest priority for women who are battered is reported to be "to get away temporarily"[138] and transition houses are the only viable alternative for many women, these houses are not given ample public and governmental recognition or support. They are run by dedicated people who work for wages which are almost always too low, and for hours that are too long. Almost all houses must rely significantly on volunteer help. But dedication alone cannot

[138] From interviews with transition houses, and from Hilberman and Munson. *op. cit.*

TABLE II

NUMBER OF CANADIAN TRANSITION HOUSES & HOSTELS FOR WOMEN WHO HAVE BEEN BATTERED BY PROVINCE, AS OF DECEMBER 1979.

Province/ Territory	No. of Houses Currently in Operation	No. of Houses Planned to Open in 1980
Newfoundland	0	1
Prince Edward Island	0	0
New Brunswick	3	0
Nova Scotia	1	0
Quebec	22	5
Ontario	29	2
Manitoba	2	0
Saskatchewan	3	1
Alberta	2	1
British Columbia	9	0
Yukon	0	1
Northwest Territories	0	1

erase the barriers which the houses continually face. In our conversations with houseworkers they enumerated many obstacles to successful operation. Three problem areas headed their lists:

Funding Mechanisms and Restrictions

Funding is unpredictable, not uniform even within one city, and always scarce. Most houses rely for their funding on a combination of provincial/local welfare money, short-term grants from federal departments, and charitable or private donations (including money through the United Way). Welfare money is not intended to support the houses themselves, but rather to provide emergency survival funds for the women who stay at the houses. This funding source is referred to as "per diem" funding. That is, for each woman who stays at the house and is eligible for welfare a fixed amount will be paid for her room and board. The per diem allotment is negotiated for each house individually and varies considerably among the houses we interviewed. The allotment is negotiated between the houseworkers and the government officials and is purportedly based on cost of housing, food, etc., in the area in which the house is located. Although houseworkers rarely complained about the per diem received, the rationality of the formula was often hard to piece together, since per diems varied from $3.75 for one house in Ontario to $18.58 for one house in the Maritimes. While the per diems are not intended to support the houses, the unpredictability and shortage of funds from other sources force most houses to depend on this steady income for their survival. Police officers and social service agency personnel are aware of the houses' dependence on this source of funding. The result is that women who are not eligible for welfare, because they have jobs, or have some savings or come from the wrong geographic area to fall under the local welfare office's jurisdiction will probably not be referred to the house. They will be forced then to return home or use limited funds to stay in a hotel or

49

another environment which provides no emotional support. If the women come to the house directly, the houses will almost always accept them if there is room whether or not they are eligible for welfare, but the houses are then forced to stretch their inadequate budgets even tighter to support extra women with the funds provided for those women who fulfill the welfare service's criteria.

By limiting women "eligible" for help to women who are "eligible" for assistance, welfare agencies force houses to restrict their services in ways which can compromise their goals. In Nova Scotia, for instance, a woman's welfare eligibility depends on whether her husband or father (if she is not married) has lived in the province for the past twelve months. Because the houses, to collect per diems and so to survive, are forced to accept primarily women eligible for welfare, they are forced to adhere to a rule which defines a woman's economic status in terms of her affiliation to her husband or father. Similarly, status Indian women who leave the reserve often find that they are not free to leave an abusive husband because of jurisdictional rulings attached to funding arrangements. Once they leave the reserve, they may not be funded by Indian Affairs, but provincial and local social services may state that status Indian women are not their responsibility. The result is that too frequently these women are given money only to return to the reserve and so to the husband they were trying to escape.

Other stipulations frequently imposed by provincial funding sources include:

- restrictions on the length of time a woman can stay in a house. Again there are variations within provinces, but a generous arrangement would be that women with children can stay 30 days maximum while a woman without children can stay one week only. In one house the maximum stay for any woman was only four days;

- demands that only women referred by government agencies and services be accepted;

- requirements for extensive monthly billing forms: a time-consuming job which can increase the pressure on severely overworked staff.

The Federal government has no specific program of support for transition houses. However, grants are available from the Women's Programme, Department of the Secretary of State, for publicity and information projects, and from Canada Works, Canada Employment and Immigration Commission, for salaries of one or more staff members. Both have a time limitation of one year, although transition houses can re-apply. National Health and Welfare, through its demonstration grants, can fund the development of a transition house to demonstrate need and a viable model of response. This is limited to a three year period and available only to new and innovative projects. In addition to these federal grants, CMHC provides very generous low interest mortgages to a number of houses. Unfortunately, there is a possibility that this program will be phased out in the coming fiscal year.

Many houses become members of the United Way to augment their per diem payments with another reliable funding source. However, stipulations are also imposed by this affiliation. Again there is variation from house to house and province to province, but in general houses which are members of the United

Way are not permitted to organize fund-raising drives, in some cases the maximum stay allowed may be reduced to less than the time limits stipulated by provincial or local governments, and in other cases only women with children are permitted residence. In addition, United Way funding, like per diem money, cannot become available until the house can prove it is operational. Many houses therefore find the financial burden of the first year impossible to bear and the house is forced to fold. Help is only offered once the house has proved it is successful - a backward philosophy for a social service.

Miscellaneous city, provincial and federal grants, YWCA sponsorship, church and private donations make up the rest of the houses' funding. Some houses who do accept women who work, ask them to pay what they can towards their room and board.

Funding restrictions place unnecessary pressures on houseworkers, keep many houses from providing as global a service as they would want and leave many women with no alternative but to return home. The uncertainty of funding means that much staff time and energy must be devoted to an ongoing search for funds to keep the house in operation.

There are noticeable discrepancies among provinces in the amount of government financial support provided. Houses in British Columbia are relatively fortunate; 83% of houses there receive per diem funding and 100% receive money from the Department of Human Resources. Quebec is now supporting twelve houses while last year it supported only two. Although the greatest number of houses exist in Ontario, provincial government support is virtually non-existent.

Lack of Official Recognition, Support and Cooperation

Lack of official recognition and support, results in a number of operational problems for the houses. A skeptical attitude towards women's shelters in the eyes of decision-makers has helped to restrict the growth of transition houses across the country. All the houses interviewed reported that they were operating at least at 100% capacity for most of the year and some, to avoid turning women away, were doubling families up in rooms where the families were willing to accept these conditions. There can be no question that more houses are needed.

Police and doctors frequently refuse to cooperate with the houses and so refuse to refer women to them. Less than 25% of the women who stayed at the houses interviewed had been referred by either the police or a hospital although these are the two most likely places a woman will first seek help.

Because of lack of adequate police protection, the women who come to the houses and the transition house workers experience unnecessary danger, both when an irate husband follows the wife to the house or discovers her there, or when the workers accompany the women to their homes without a police escort to collect their belongings.

Lack of Follow-up and Support Services

Many house workers would like to provide follow-up services for the women who stay with them. Inadequate funding and lack of public support make this desire little more than a pipe-dream. The lack of follow-up and support services most clearly demonstrates how impossible it really is for a woman to leave a husband who beats her and to survive economically and emotionally on her own.

51

There are no long-term housing alternatives for women with little money, especially if they have children. House workers reported that landlords are often hostile to single parents, there is not enough low-rent housing, an increasing number of apartment buildings do not accept children, and zoning restrictions on cooperative housing erase one of the most positive options for women who have been battered to provide financial and emotional support for each other. Further, women cannot apply for subsidized housing for themselves until they have actually separated from their husbands.

There is not enough affordable child care available to help women reintegrate - to find a place to live, to find a job, to work full-time - after their transition house stay. There is not enough good career counselling, especially career counselling which is sensitive to the special job needs of women with young children. Many women want counselling for themselves or their husbands. A type of counselling is needed, however, which will not define its primary goal as necessarily re-establishing or strengthening the family, but which will help the woman and man reach their decisions and help them learn the ways to carry out these decisions. The woman may decide to return to her husband and this decision should be respected by the counsellor; but a woman should not be counselled in such a way that she sees this as her only possible option. The counsellor should help to make her aware of as many options as possible.

As well, women reported that drop-in centres are needed, along with more family health clinics, well-woman clinics and programs for alcoholic men and women.

Transition houses are an essential service for women who have been battered. "Over and over, women who have been through the experience of leaving a violent situation identify the transition house as the most effective service the community has offered them."[139] Recognition of their value is slowly increasing. As mentioned earlier the Quebec government now sponsors twelve houses. The New Brunswick government recently provided a building in Fredericton to be used as a shelter for battered women. But the recognition grows too slowly. Some women's groups who have had to close their transition houses because of lack of funds are taking women into their own homes.

Transition houses represent a support approach to wife battering, rather than a treatment approach and so reflect the women's own perceptions of their major needs. Most houses do more than protect the woman from physical harm. They attempt to make her aware of her options and attempt to strengthen her ability to follow through on her decisions. They reflect an attempt to increase the real choices for women who have been battered in the face of a whole society which is structured to limit their choices.

Police Crisis Intervention

Other emergency services to complement or make-up for the absence of transition houses in Canada, are being developed by some police departments. As we detailed earlier, most of the transition houses interviewed identified police crisis intervention as a general and persistent problem, either because the police had not been trained to deal with wife battering incidents or because they would not always refer women to the houses.

Some police departments across the country have shared this recognition of how crucial sensitive police intervention can be in cases of domestic violence, and have instituted special training programs or crisis intervention units to dispatch for such cases. Levens and Dutton, in their extensive work on legal intervention in

[139] MacLeod, Flora, op. cit., p. 9.

cases of family violence, stress the importance of cooperation between the police and various other agencies in effectively dealing with wife battering:

> It is clear that our society's inadequate response to acts of marital violence is in part due to the fragmentation of existing resources. There is a manifest need for coherent policies that include and coordinate supportive police work, innovative legal procedures and a nucleus of persons capable of employing the techniques and insights of the social professions.[140]

[140] Levens, op. cit., p. 42.

This philosophy is reflected in the crisis intervention units which are in operation in Canada.

The Mobile Family Service Society.

In 1972 the Mobile Family Service Society was created in Regina, Saskatchewan. Its goal was to provide 24-hour crisis intervention services for Regina in crisis situations of all types, and to provide referral for follow-up services. It is accessible by phone through its own line, through other crisis lines across the city, through the emergency number for the Department of Social Services, through the child abuse line, and through the police department switchboard, although it is not a part of the police department, as are some crisis intervention services.

It is operated by a number of service agencies which formerly provided separate, relatively uncoordinated services to people with a variety of domestic problems. In 1976/77, 26 agencies were represented. This Service Society grew out of a police training course in crisis intervention and the increased awareness of the importance of coordination which this course instilled in the police.

A study to evaluate the effectiveness of this program, found that response time for each call dropped from 14 minutes to 7 minutes between 1975-76 and 1976-77, and 42% of the people who contacted the Service are self-referred so that the use of the police as a middle agency has diminished.

"If we assume that the overall usage of a service by the public is a measure of the relevance and credibility of the service, then Mobile Family is being successful in creating a favourable climate for reporting." Over three years, demands for help have tripled. It is also worth noting that the Regina Transition House was established by two of the original staff of the Mobile Family Program.[141]

[141] Bell in Eekelaar & Katz, op. cit., p. 212-214.

The London, Ontario, Family Consultant Service

This service also developed in 1972 out of a police training program, to assist police officers in dealing with domestic disputes - by intervening in crisis situations at the officers' request, by arranging referrals to appropriate social agencies and by providing training for police officers in crisis intervention. The Family Consultants are five professionals - a nurse, a legal expert, a feminist counsellor, a clinical psychologist and a social worker who operate directly out of the London Police Department 19 hours a day on weekdays and 14 hours a day on weekends, including the crucial four hours past midnight. Like the Regina Mobile Family Service Society, the crises they deal with range from wife battering to alcohol and drug abuse, although the most frequent type of cases handled are "family or marital dispute cases".[142]

[142] Ibid., p. 219.

The Women's Community House, a transition house in London, Ontario, reports that police co-operation and referrals have been high since the Family Consultant Service was implemented - 40.5% of the women who come to their house are referred by the police. The average for other houses which collected this information was less than 15%.

Edmonton Family Court Conciliation Service

This service has helped wives who are battered assess the options opern to them. If they choose to stay with or return to their husbands they are referred for long-term counselling; legal advice is given if they decide to leave.

Edmonton does not support the idea of a mobile unit of social workers, but instead trains all officers in crisis intervention and assigns police to do follow-up and referral.

Calgary Squabble Squad

This squad has its own unmarked cars and police radios and is on call around the clock. It is headed by the former head of the Calgary Rape Crisis Centre and is modelled after the London, Ontario, consultant service.[143]

[143] *The Calgary Herald,* October 22, 1979.

B.C. Intervention Services

Two mobile units presently exist in Vancouver - the "Godsquad", a travelling team in North Vancouver consisting of a police officer trained in handling domestic disputes and a member of the clergy; and Car 86, a similar team made up of a police officer and a social worker. These units, unlike the earlier models set up in London and Regina, are restricted to incidents of family violence.

Police Training Programs

Programs designed to improve the way police deal with family disputes are also increasing.

Where Are They Located?

• The Canadian Police College in Ottawa which trains officers who will themselves become trainers in their local area, offered a two-week program on domestic dispute intervention in June 1979 and again in December 1979.

• British Columbia has done extensive evaluation studies on the merits of training police in family crisis intervention. Since 1976 the Police Academy course has included six days training in family crisis intervention.

• In Alberta, police officers in Calgary and Edmonton are given some training in family crisis intervention. In Edmonton, since September 1979, every nine-week recruit training program has included eight hours instruction on intervention in domestic disputes. After two years of service, every officer is given a one-week course on human relations which includes discussion of the problems of battered wives. In addition there are four detectives who perform follow-up visits, give referrals and can provide some counselling after the initial crisis intervention. Reports are written for every case whether or not charges are to be laid.

• The Saskatchewan police college also provides a section on family crisis intervention.

- Manitoba, through its police college in Winnipeg gives all recruits eight hours of classroom instruction and eight hours of practice exercises in family crisis intervention.

- Ontario provides no training in crisis intervention at the recruit level but does offer a four-day course to supervisors.

- The Institut de police du Québec has integrated information on family violence and how to deal with it in several of its courses; role-playing sessions form a central part of its approach.

- In New Brunswick and Prince Edward Island, police deal very little with the topic of battered wives and crisis intervention in any of their training courses.

- In Nova Scotia the Halifax police school offers only one seminar specifically for family crisis intervention in a six-month training period.

- In Newfoundland, all police officers are given a course in domestic disputes which involves training in referrals and report-writing as well as immediate intervention.

The Value of Police Training

An Official Evaluation

Levens and Dutton have done five major evaluation studies on the effects of police training in domestic crisis intervention. They found that trained officers were slightly more likely than untrained officers (21% compared to 18%) to remove one of the parties from the home to protect the safety of the victim. Trained officers were also twice as likely to refer the wife and/or husband to another social agency. Untrained officers were more than twice as likely to lay charges and to refer the woman who had been battered to a Justice of the Peace for a peace order. Trained officers tended to take a counselling role.

The Woman's Point of View

From the point of view of the woman who has been battered, the fact that police trained in crisis intervention are more likely to refer her to a transition house near her satisfies her major reported priority. For those few cases of family violence where counselling is desired by the husband as well as the wife, the approach of these intervention units is also highly beneficial. A surface look at these programs suggests however that for most of the units, counselling, and so individualized treatment, takes precedence over a more global support program. While we do not want to denounce all counselling programs or deny the need for individual treatment in some cases, the fact that the basic premise of most counselling is to look inward and to attempt to reunite the family makes the value of this approach questionable in ensuring the protection of the woman and in meeting her needs, as these needs are defined by women who have been battered. This conclusion of course can remain speculative only, given the absence of evaluative studies of these programs from the point of view of women who have been battered, and the absence of a closer look at how support and information-oriented the counselling services are.

Legal Initiatives in Canada

- The New Brunswick government, in response to a recommendation made by the New Brunswick Advisory Council on the Status of Women that mandatory reporting of child abuse and neglect be extended to require the reporting of all forms of family violence, announced its intention to include such provisions in the law in the future.

• On May 1, 1978, former Liberal Justice Minister Ron Basford introduced amendments to the existing laws on sexual offences, which would emphasize the violence attached to rape rather than the sexual aspect and which would apply to sexual assault between spouses as long as they were living separate and apart.[144] His successor, Conservative Justice Minister Jacques Flynn announced in October 1979 that he intended to totally remove the spousal exemption that prohibits a husband or wife from charging the other with rape.[145]

[144] Goldman, *op. cit.*, p. 32.

[145] *The Globe and Mail*, 1979, p. 1, October 12.

Other Government Initiatives

• The Quebec government launched a series of consultations across the province between October 1979 and January 1980 to bring together representatives from the police, the justice system and social service agencies, including transition houses, to raise awareness about the problem of wife battering and to begin discussions on more effective approaches to deal with the problem. A provincial symposium will be held in 1980, based on the findings of these consultations, to draw formal recommendations.

The United Way Initiatives

• The United Way, which provides some of the sustaining funding for transition houses across Canada, organized a two-year task force which grew out of the United Way-sponsored symposium on family violence in the spring of 1977. Representatives of the women's movement, including several members of the Vancouver Status of Women, were included on the task force and had a strong influence on the recommendations included in the final report released in the fall of 1979.

The U.S. Response to Wife Battering

Although the first Canadian transition house specifically for women who had been battered pre-dated the first U.S. house by two years, recent activity in the U.S. has been much more organized and forceful than in Canada and has focused primarily on legal reforms. The Pennsylvania legislature has passed a law giving judges the power to evict violent spouses from their homes for up to one year without the wives having to press criminal charges. The New York City Police Department has agreed to arrest men who beat their wives, waiving former practices whereby some police officers would refuse to arrest these men because it was a family situation or because the woman had not been to family court.

A Domestic Violence Prevention and Services Act was passed by the House of Representatives in mid-December, 1979, and is now under consideration by the Senate. This Act will make available special grants for the Department of Health, Education and Welfare to allot to individual states in order to assist in the establishment of shelters for battered wives. There will also be media campaigns on domestic violence that will tell the women where they can go for help, and where they should call. A national clearinghouse within the Department of Education is also to be established. This office will give information on current research, grant assistance and will generally answer inquiries and organise information concerning wife battering. In addition, an Office on Domestic Violence was established in the summer of 1979 in the Department of Health, Education and Welfare to co-ordinate research, service programs and other HEW activities related to spouse abuse. Finally, the Department of Housing and Urban Development has approved the use of funds to acquire and rehabilitate buildings which will become group homes, halfway houses and emergency shelters.

While the U.S. initiatives may not provide the model Canada will want to follow, the emphasis on co-ordinated support for transition houses combined with regional responsibility and extensive public awareness programs does provide a forceful route to consider for implementation in Canada.

CHAPTER VIII

WHAT REMAINS TO BE DONE

What Do Women Who Are Battered Really Want?

While the need for action is undeniable, careful consideration of the expressions of what women who are battered really want is imperative if their needs are to be met. Some may argue that this is a biased view, but it appears from our work on the subject that it is the voices of women who have been battered that have most often been ignored.

Women who have been battered above all want immediate physical protection for themselves and their children. After or preferably along with protection they want emotional support - they want to know they're not alone, that there are people who know what it's like to be battered, know the confusion and hopelessness they feel, feelings that usually eclipse their pain and anger. And they want things to be all right again - they want their lives to be put back in order, to have time to arrange their futures. To truly help women who have been battered, we must look closely at what they really want, at what these statements really mean and avoid imposing an interpretation that does not reflect the women's experiences.

Of course, not all women want the same result. Some women want to return to their husbands, to give the relationship another chance. Others want to be as far away from their husbands as possible, and are mentally and physically prepared to support themselves and their children. But most don't know what they ultimately want in explicit, action terms They have been beaten physically but also mentally be their husbands and by their lack of options - they want to do something but the possibilities aren't clear. They want a chance to rest, to talk, to think things over and sort things out in their minds. They do know what they want immediately but they don't know where to get it - often because what they want simply does not exist. Many women who have been beaten expressed what their priorities were very clearly in the survey done in Thunder Bay and gave intimations of what had been wrong with the help they had received in the past. For example:

> • *(The husband) should be detained and not be left in the house after abuse. Women tend to shelter children and need time to arrange the future, courts should be more strict, Children's Aid should not make demands on wives to keep home and quit working, without seeing the husband does support as he claims. There is no follow-up. Counselling should be done by very experienced staff.*

> • *Women need to know and understand how to seek help for themselves.*

> • *Crisis shelters and a 24-hour crisis line are desperately needed.*

> • *I think there should be some kind of a women's center...where women can meet, discuss their problems and share ideas. Where a woman can be helped when seeking information on many subjects related to women, such as birth control, abortion, rape, physical abuse and legal advice... Women need to stick together.*

> • *Maybe if they were helped by others they might be able to help themselves.*

> • *Family court isn't too good because judges are men and men stick together.*

• *Detective_____informed my sister that he believed the incident didn't occur. Maybe this is why some women don't report it. It is usually believed the woman is at fault all the time.*

• *There should be somewhere where women can go to and the spouses or partners should be charged the first time it happens. Not let it pass time and time again without anything being done. A lot of women are wasting their time 'trying to lay charges the first time' because nothing is ever done about it.*

• *More education for women on how to handle the situation when it happens. Someone or something to give her the strength to leave. Try to take away the fear.* [146]

[146] All quotes taken from *Women in Transition, op. cit.*

Women who have been battered want to be listened to. They want their ideas, plans and requests for help taken seriously, they do not want to be told they are crazy or that they have made their husbands beat them or that it's up to them to try harder. They can hear these messages from their husbands, and they know or at least suspect that these verdicts are not true.

To provide the support women who are battered say they need, action is required on several levels: emergency services, support services, legal support, and long-range prevention. Suggestions for action where the source is not acknowledged are derived primarily from our interviews with transition houses.

Emergency Services

The incidence and severity of wife battering make twenty-four hour emergency services and refuges across the country the top priority for immediate action. This priority is almost universally recognized and has been explicitly recommended by such groups as the United Way and Conseil du statut de la femme, as well as most authors on the subject of wife abuse. A comprehensive, reliable, sustaining funding mechanism is needed for houses in existence - a mechanism which does not compromise the autonomy of the houses, does not force workers to live on inadequate wages or force them to restrict their house to certain types of women in order to receive their full funding. Funds should also be provided generously for houses currently in the planning stages and to promote the creation of new houses, particularly in areas where women have no access to transition houses. Many of the houses interviewed repeatedly emphasized the problems they had experienced getting started. To receive funds to begin the service, the women were frequently told they had to prove a service was needed in the area and the only acceptable proof cited was statistics on the numbers of women coming to them for help - statistics which could only be provided if the house were operational. New transition houses should not be thwarted because of this "Catch 22" situation. Out figures indicate that wife battering exists across Canada - it is very unlikely that there are any villages, towns, cities or provinces which are potentially free of this form of family violence. The need has been demonstrated. Funding should not be withheld on the excuse that "It doesn't happen here".

Co-ordinated services are imperative - women need transition houses first and foremost, but the aid transition houses provide will be most effective if accessible crisis centers are also established to provide comprehensive financial, legal and medical assistance on an emergency 24-hour basis.

In a 1976 review, the United Way of Greater Vancouver elaborates on this need and the roles such a crisis center could assume.

The crisis centers should have three primary roles:

> *First, they should provide emergency services. This is the provision of an intitial contact on a 24-hour basis, immediate emergency counselling on rights and services available, and assistance for women to leave dangerous home situations. Emergency services require close liaison with local medical, social, legal and police services. Second, they should be responsible for co-ordinating existing arrangements for families in distress. This requires bringing those in need into contact with lawyer, doctor, health visitor, housing and financial services, clergyman, probation officer, marriage guidance counsellor, child care worker, and so on. Third, the centre should be responsible for the development of specialist advisory services, education and publicity programs, group support for women with similar problems, and the recording of data on incidence, treatment and outcome.[147]*

[147] Downey, Joanne, & Howell, Jane, *Wife Battering: A Review and Preliminary Enquiry into Local Incidence, Needs and Resources*, United Way of Greater Vancouver, Vancouver, B.C., 1976, p. 1.

Until community crisis centers are established where services are geographically co-ordinated, efficient communication networks are needed between the police, transition houses and counselling services. The success of the communication network established in London, Ontario serves as an example of the workability of this idea. Many houses have also mentioned the need for the provision of funds for more services within the transition houses themselves. For example, Lenny Untinen, who helped co-ordinate *Women in Transition* which has been quoted so extensively throughout this report, recommended that funding be available for the employment of non-traditional counsellors - i.e. counsellors who by their experience and background can empathize with their clients. Many houses also stressed the need for more services for the children who stay in the houses, including child-care, recreational services and counselling.

Support Services

Crisis intervention, no matter how effective, can never provide women who are battered with the support they need to make responsible decisions about the course of action they will take. Various support services are needed to back up crisis intervention and to provide the continuity necessary. These support services could include what the United Way task force calls "second-stage housing"[148] - housing outside the transition house which still incorporates the emotional, physical and child-care support which was provided by the transition house. The most likely model for this form of housing would be a co-operative where women who had been battered could stay until they felt they could manage on their own or had made other firm decisions for future action. The co-operative should be located fairly close to the transition house and to the crisis center to provide aid and/or protection if these became necessary.

[148] MacLeod, Flora, *op. cit.*, p. 10.

Zoning changes in many areas would be required to allow for the formation of these cooperatives.

If wife battering is seen as a process rooted in the structure of our institutions rather than just as isolated incidents, the long-term needs of women who have been battered, of their children and also of their husbands, become apparent, whether or not the women leave their husbands. Child care is a top priority to allow the woman to pursue legal alternatives, to look for a job, to find a new home, or just to provide time for her to think things through. In the cases where alcohol is a precipitating factor, attendance at Alcoholics Anonymous meetings or other forms of counselling (where agreed to) should be supported. Decisions about legal actions may change and delays in legal processes can be confusing and frustrating. Ongoing legal counsel is needed. Children may need recreational outlets or counselling support. Women may need drop-in centers and social clubs to make new friends, to feel accepted. Where men who batter are willing to accept counselling, such assistance should be provided. Women who decide to leave their husbands may need career counselling, retraining, or help in dealing with the welfare system. Immigrant women should be offered language training. One innovative Ottawa woman, realizing the need for language training among immigrant women and of the difficulties many of them experienced in leaving the house because of family responsibilities or the disapproval of their husbands, offered language training over the telephone.

Support services must be imaginative and flexible and provide help to women who have been battered. Whether they choose to go back to their husbands or to leave them, they will need the emotional and information support and the help which these services would provide.

Follow-up support services can also become preventive services. If sufficient child-care, career counselling, feminist counselling services, etc. were available and accessible to all women, their isolation and dependence would diminish and so hopefully would wife battering.

> *The women who use refuges still have as their major problem how to live in the long run, either with or without their husbands. At the moment there is virtually no systematic knowledge of what happens to women after they leave refuges, and yet this must be crucial in deciding what policies to adopt. We need to know how women who return to their husbands fare; whether there is an uneasy and sullen truce, whether violence starts again after a while, or whether the shock has made the husband appreciate his wife rather more than he did? Could any counselling be attempted and, if so, did it help? Conversely, if there is a final separation what price do the wife and her children have to pay in the form of difficulties and reduced standard of living; who gives help and what is most effective; how does she cope with her shattered morale and problems of identity as a woman? Such questions badly need to be answered if all the care and energy put into the provision of refuges is to lead to other programs which in the end help prevent violence.*[149]

149 Martin, J.P., "Family Violence and Social Policy" in Martin, J.P., *op. cit.*, p. 243.

Legal Reform

Sides are most clearly drawn on the issue of legal reform. Although there is almost universal agreement on the need for more transition houses, better funding mechanisms, more support services, and better crisis intervention, the role of the law in the process of wife battering is a much more problematic area.

The extremes polarize around the issues of non-arrest, arrest and special treatment for cases of family dispute versus generalization of the law to eliminate special treatment in family cases.

The Law Reform Commission of Canada represents the first position. It recommended in 1976 that:

> *police departments encourage the screening out of family disputes from the criminal process and that prosecutors attempt pre-trial settlements of cases involving a prior relationship between the victim and the offender.*[150]

150 Goldman, *op. cit.*, cited on p. 162.

This position is also essentially supported in the Crisis Intervention Units set up by police departments across Canada.

> In general, legal officials view spousal assault as domestic dispute, disruptions of civil order rather than infractions of criminal law, with the result that few wife-batterers are charged or arrested.[151]

[151] Aldridge, James R., et al. "Battered Wives and the Justice System", paper prepared for Dr. John Hogarth, Faculty of Law, University of British Columbia, fall 1978, p. 11.

Others however strongly dispute this position:

> In spite of the strong evidence that minor disputes left unchecked may escalate, the scholarly literature on new policy methods makes no mention of factors that indicate the need for prompt arrest instead of mediation. The emphasis is on the trivial nature of family disputes and calming the participants.
>
> These assumptions were made from the point of view of the police officers who were the subject of the researchers. When battered wives were studied, however, the conclusion was that the police are called by wives who are severely abused and that the response is ineffective.[152]

[152] Fields, Marjory D., "Representing Battered Wives, or What to Do Until the Police Arrive" in the Family Law Reporter, Monograph No. 25, April 5, 1977, p. 3.

These arguments have led to a second stance, i.e. that arrest in some cases should be the general policy, so that the attacker is removed from the situation. The United Way, for example, made the following recommendations in support of this position:

> – that police send help whenever a woman calls and says her husband has assaulted or threatened her, arrest the husband in all cases where a court order has been violated and assist victims of wife battering in other ways such as obtaining medical help.
>
> – that police authorities in B.C. enforce a policy of arresting men who commit serious assault against their wives so long as there is reasonable cause to believe that a crime has been committed.
>
> – that police arrest a person in less serious assault cases as they would in cases in which the parties were not married to each other.[153]

[153] MacLeod, Flora, op. cit., p. 10.

In other words, the position which calls for arrest in some cases is asking that wives be given the same legal rights against assault by their husbands in their homes as they would be given if a stranger assaulted them outside the home.

This position has also been strongly supported by some judges and lawyers in the United States. For example, Raymond Parnas, a professor at the School of Law, University of California, states:

> The criminal law, the police, the prosecutor and the courts should not only continue to respond to incidents of interspousal violence but should emphasize the importance of the traditional response of arrest, prosecution and sanction as a sign of public disapprobation and protection, not only at the upper levels of violence, but also at the first minimal signs of trouble.[154]

[154] Parnas, Raymond I., "The Relevance of Criminal Law to Interspousal Violence", in Eekelaar & Katz, op. cit., p. 191.

However, critics of this approach cite historical examples of the failure of legislative attempts to stop wife beating. Michael Freeman, for example, points out that in England and Maryland in the 1880's, laws were posted demanding that wife beaters be flogged. The result was a wave of punitive wife beating by irate husbands.[155]

[155] Freeman, Michael, "Le vice anglais? - Wife Battering in English and American Law", Family Law Quarterly, Vol. XI, No. 3, fall 1977, p. 200.

In England in 1853, under the "Act for the Better Prevention and Punishment of Aggravated Assaults Upon Women and Children", magistrates were empowered to summarily punish those convicted of aggravated assaults on women and males under 14 with up to 6 months' imprisonment, with or without hard labour, or a fine of up to £20 with similar imprisonment on default, and additionally bind them over to keep the peace for 6 months. More expeditious justice, it was hoped, would encourage the victims to complain and deter brutal husbands.[156] In fact, however, the result of these harsh sentences was that few complaints and fewer arrests were made.

156 May, Margaret, "Violence in the Family: an Historical Perspective", in Martin, J.P., op. cit., p. 144.

One innovative act in 1878 - the Matrimonial Causes Act, with its power to award wives a judicial separation, custody of children under ten, and maintenance where the husband had been convicted of an aggravated assault, and with its significant emphasis on safeguarding and maintaining the wife - did have a very pronounced if delayed effect. Although at first few women claimed their rights, when the grounds for cruelty were expanded to include persistent cruelty and wilful neglect, there was a flood of applications.[157]

157 Ibid., p. 149.

These historical lessons provide some direction. They point out that legislation which is strictly punitive, which does not take into account the economic and political realities of the situation and which is not accompanied by an attempt to provide support for the victim, is probably doomed to be ineffective. This corresponds to our findings. Most wives are loath to send their husbands to jail, and most judges avoid such a sentence, because at worst the husband may return to the wife and inflict retributive violence, or at best the husband will return and things will return to "normal" - a normalcy which often includes violence. In the interim, while the husband is in jail, the family is frequently deprived of its major source of income. Jail terms and fines are therefore punitive for the victim as well as the accused.

Arrest policies in a vacuum, without complementary changes in other legal procedures both pre-and post-arrest, can have the same effect. Even if the man does not receive a severe sentence, the arrest can provoke anger which can in turn provoke violence. An arrest policy supported by only token sentences or regular dismissals would quickly become an aggravation for police who have to make the arrest and would lapse into non-use. An arrest policy supported by jail terms would quickly require a string of new jails. A simple punitive approach does not appear to be a viable answer.

Yet it cannot be denied that the law plays an important role in shaping societal attitudes and behaviour. If violence within the home is to become unacceptable to men and women across Canada, some reform of the law is needed. This reform can best be achieved by increasing the rights of wives and support given to women under the system through a coordinated approach to legislative change and policy change. Legislative change which could be considered includes the deletion of spousal immunity in rape cases, which has already been proposed by Conservative Justice Minister Flynn; allowing spouses to sue each other (a recommendation made at an April 1978 conference entitled "Women in a Violent Society") and requiring third parties who have knowledge of wife battering to report it (Shea & Derogen and the New Brunswick Advisory Council on the Status of Women). Changes in the policies which determine the way law officers (police, lawyers, justices of the peace and judges) actually implement the law are much more significant, however. Such policies would include:

- referring women who are battered to transition houses in all cases;
- contacting social service personnel to obtain immediate emergency financial assistance;
- carrying through with arrests and sentencing when the woman does press charges;
- not imposing trial reconciliation periods on couples prior to granting a divorce;
- accepting evidence of past assault as permissible evidence in an assault case between husband and wife;
- ensuring that police training in domestic disputes does not emphasize reconciliation where this is not the desire of the parties;
- allowing a woman to apply for an injunction whether or not she is also applying for a divorce;
- instructing police to accompany women to the marital home to collect their belongings.

This list of possible changes in legal policy can be incorporated into a three-part model of legal change. This model would be based on the following five principles:

1. The law must be used to convey the message that assault is a crime whether it occurs within or outside the home.
2. The law must provide protection for victims of assault
3. Legal procedures should be designed as much as possible to reflect the best interests of the woman who is battered, her husband and their children. (For example, it is usually not in the best interests of the wife, the husband or their children for the husband to lose his job because he has been put in jail.)
4. The woman who has been battered should receive as much information as possible on her legal options and their implications.
5. The informed opinion of the woman who has been battered as to the most appropriate legal option should be taken into account when the case is dealt with.

The three parts of a general model based on these principles might include:

1. A clear, publicly advertised policy applying the same standards of arrest/non-arrest to family violence as to assault outside the family;
2. If the husband is arrested, immediately after arrest, a victim advocate service - independent of, but with direct access to, the criminal justice system - could be called to inform the wife of the options available to her, to explain their consequences, discuss her financial alternatives, and then, on the basis of this information, ask the woman to recommend the most appropriate sentencing or pre-sentencing release options for her case. Her informed opinion would then be relayed to the judge.

A program of this type has been developed in Pima County, Arizona. Women who have been battered are asked to suggest conditions of the husband's pre-sentence release. The coordinator of the program reports that "Battered women have been very practical about the conditions…they would like…Consequently judges have been receptive to their wishes and have usually complied."[158] Under this program the Victim Witness Advocate staff keeps the woman informed of her legal status and options until the case is finally decided. In addition, staff members escort her to court and arrange day care if this is needed.

[158] Martin Del, "Battered Women: Society's Problem" in Chapman, J.R., & Gates, M., eds., *The Victimization of Women*, Sage, Beverly Hills, 1978, p. 135.

3. An expanded range of options would be developed both for sentencing after conviction (so the judge would not be limited to fines and jail terms, neither of which tend to be in the best interests of the women or their husbands) and also for pre-trial release.

This model would ensure that the voice of the woman who is battered is heard, and would attack some of the present inconsistencies in legal procedure which produce weak policies.

Even comprehensive reform in the legal system, however, must be supported by reforms in other institutions if long-range prevention of family violence is to be a realizable goal.

Long-Range Prevention

Programs for long-range prevention are of course the most challenging. If wife battering is ever to be significantly reduced, the structures, practices, traditions and beliefs which keep women dependent and isolated within the family and which keep the family outside legal and public censure, must be gradually erased. Long-range prevention requires at least three basic types of programs: programs which will help promote the economic independence of women, education and training, and information collection and research.

Education is an urgent and overwhelming need. We have cited studies which show the extent to which wife battering is taught to be a legitimate process. Education includes increasing the general awareness of the public about the incidence, severity and characteristics of wife beating. It also includes education in public and highschools on the laws surrounding family life, the value, use and availability of social services, as well as presentation of family models which do not perpetuate an image of the woman as dependent, but rather present women in a wide variety of roles.

Women in all situations need specific local education programs on what their rights and alternatives are if they are beaten. The realities of violence must be emphasized to dispel myths that the woman deserves to be beaten, or it's natural for men to be aggressive, and so encourage women to share their problems instead of hiding them behind guilt and self-blame. Courses should be offered in native languages to immigrants as well as Canada's native people.

Professionals who deal with women who are battered must be given training programs to sensitize them to the experiences and emotions of the woman who is battered, to alert them to the built-in isolation of the woman which our legal, medical and social systems perpetuate, and to emphasize the protective and supportive roles which are needed. Professionals should be made aware of cross-disciplinary aspects of the problem. So for example, a doctor should be aware of the legal dimensions of wife beating and the policeman should have some knowledge of the severity of the injuries that frequently result. A more ambitious approach, but a necessary one nonetheless, is to revise textbooks used by medical, legal and social work students wherever possible to reduce unfounded negative images of women.

While information collection and research is not as immediately vital as some of the other areas of reform, it is essential to increase knowledge and understanding of the problem if the severity of the problem is to be fully accepted throughout our society. Studies are needed to evaluate the short and long-term effects of various treatment models on different family members; more research should involve people who have worked with women who have been battered; longitudinal studies are needed to better understand patterns of wife battering; and policy-oriented research should be a high priority.

An integrated information collection system could be instituted among hospital emergency staff, doctors, lawyers, police, transition house workers and other professionals who come in contact with women who have been battered. A mandatory system of reporting similar to that in place for child abuse should be considered.

Finally, steps to increase the economic independence of women must be taken to reduce the isolation and dependence of women. These steps should include enforcing equal pay for work of equal value legislation, improving pension and other fringe benefits available to women, increasing the integration between the family and the work place through more affordable and more widely accessible child care, flexible work hours and parental leave allowances. Without economic independence, women will continue to be seen by many as second-class citizens and so "legitimate" victims.

A Final Word

The victimization of married women who are assaulted by their husbands goes beyond their physical battering. Wife battering is much more than individual cases of physical violence. It is the license society gives a man to use violence against his wife without fear of retribution - he may never take this license, but he possesses it nonetheless. The license is enforced through a system of restrictions imposed on married women - restrictions which can imprison a woman in a violent marriage against her will and which implicitly condone the violent behaviour of her husband.

The bars of her prison are often invisible. A few are explicit and are publicly known, like the law which prevents a wife from charging her husband with rape. Others however - like the doctor's unwillingness to listen, like the woman's inability to provide economic support for herself and her children, like her friend's attitude that "her husband's really a nice guy and she should try harder to be a good wife" - are usually invisible. They are rarely discovered until a crisis like a physical beating leads the wife to consider alternative sources of economic and emotional support. Most women never dream - until they are physically battered - that if they need help, the likelihood is that no-one will come.

Wife battering is not one problem - it is many tangled problems. Wife battering is undeniably a health problem; many women have been permanently disabled from attacks by their husbands, others have endured a brutal death.

But the pain women experience from their physical injuries is often minor in comparison to the painful shock they receive when they call for help only to find that their legal and civil rights and even their credibility as people stop at the threshold of the marital home.

Wife battering is therefore also a legal problem. The law supports wife battering through archaic ordinances and ineffective procudures. It is a civil rights problem: married women who are battered find their freedom of choice is severely curtailed.

In addition wife battering is an economic problem. Because the work of women in the home is given no financial recognition and the work of women outside the home is usually poorly paid, many women who are beaten do not have the option to leave, especially if they have children to support.

Finally, wife battering is an educational problem. About one in ten married women - that's approximately 500,000 women - are battered each year in Canada, and yet no-one talks about wife battering. The majority of women who are battered don't even realize there are other women who share their experiences. And what about the children in homes where the wife is battered? They learn from first-hand experience that violence is acceptable behaviour. They see outsiders take their father's side, they often join the majority and turn against their mother. They learn to accept women as appropriate victims of violence within the family.

Any significant decrease in the incidence of wife battering is only possible if coordinated and imaginative approaches to all these aspects of the problem are initiated.

Easy and quick solutions cannot be found and the temptation must be resisted to look for change first in individuals or in particular families. Not even attacks against "marriage" will provide constructive directions. Women and men need the emotional support and closeness which families of various types, including marriage, can provide.

The object of attack instead must be the rules, traditions and policies of institutions which support a particular form of the family - a form based on the woman's unquestioned inequality - a form which strains the potential for support and closeness between marriage partners. New rules, procedures and family roles are needed which do not encourage marital homes to become battle fields. Women and men need the real choice to live in families without violence.

APPENDIX "A"

TRANSITION HOUSES BY PROVINCE ACROSS CANADA*

*Note: At their request, some of the transition houses that submitted information for this report are not included in this Appendix

BRITISH COLUMBIA

Coquitlam Women's
Transition House
Port Coquitlam, B.C.
464-2020 (604)
524-4444 after hours

Ishtar Transition House
Langley, B.C.
530-9442 (604)

Owl House Society
Vancouver, B.C.
873-8114 (604)

Powell Place Sanctuary for
Women
Vancouver, B.C.
683-0919 (604)

Surrey Emergency Shelter
Surrey, B.C.
588-7446 (604)

The Burnaby Emergency
Shelter for Women and
Children
Burnaby, B.C.
291-1218, 291-1219 (604)

Vancouver Transition
House
Vancouver, B.C.
874-5116 (604)

Vernon Women's
Transition House
Vernon, B.C.
542-1473 (604)

Victoria Women's
Transition House
Victoria, B.C.
385-6611 (604)

ALBERTA

Calgary Women's
Emergency Shelter
Calgary, Alta.
245-4442 (403)

WIN House
Edmonton, Alta.
479-0058 (403)

SASKATCHEWAN

Interval House
Saskatoon, Sask.
244-0185 (306)

Regina Native Women's
Residence and Resource
Center
Regina, Sask.
545-2062 (306)

Regina Transition
Women's Society
Regina, Sask.
569-2292 (306)

MANITOBA

Osborne House
Winnipeg, Man.
775-8197 (204)

Westman Women's
Shelter
Brandon, Man.
727-3644 (204)

ONTARIO

Amity House
Ottawa, Ont.
234-7204 (613)

Anselma House
Kitchener, Ont.
742-5894 (519)

Avoca House (Interval
Program)
Eganville, Ont.
628-2154 (613)

Beendigen Inc. Native
Women's Crisis House
Thunder Bay, Ont.
622-5101 (807)

Bernadette McCann
House for Women
Pembroke, Ont.
732-3131 (613)

Cambridge Rotary Family
Centre
Cambridge, Ont.
621-6830 (519)

Carleton Place Interval
House
Carleton Place, Ont.
257-5960 (613)

Community Residence
Thunder Bay, Ont.
623-2711 (807)

Family Center
London, Ont.
433-0641 (519)

Hiatus House
Windsor, Ont.
253-4458 (519)

Inasmuch House
Hamilton, Ont.
529-8149 (416)

Interval House
Toronto, Ont.
924-1491 (416)

Kenora Women's Crisis
Intervention Center
Kenora, Ont.
468-5905 (807)

Kingston Interval House
Kingston, Ont.
546-1777 (613)

Nellie's
Toronto, Ont.
461-1084 (416)

Interval House of Ottawa-
Carleton
Ottawa, Ont.
234-5181 (613)

Women's Community
House
London, Ont.
439-4543 (519)

Women's Emergency
Centre (Woodstock) Inc.
Woodstock, Ont.
539-1439 (519)

Women's Habitat
Etobicoke, (Toronto) Ont.
252-1785 (416)

Women in Crisis
Guelph, Ont.
836-5710 (519)

Women in Crisis
Sault Ste-Marie, Ont.
256-7101 (705)

Women in Transition, Inc.
Toronto, Ont.
967-5227 (416)

Women's Place
St. Catherines, Ont.
684-8331 (416)

Women's Interval Home
Sarnia, Ont.
336-5200 (519)

Y.W.C.A. Emergency
Housing
St. Thomas, Ont.
631-9800 (519)

QUÉBEC

Accueil du sans abri
Valleyfield, Que.
371-4618 (514)

Assistance aux femmes
Montréal, Que.
270-8291 (514)

Auberge Transition, Inc.
Montréal, Que.
481-0495, 481-0496 (514)

Carrefour pour elle, Inc.
Longueuil, Que.
651-5800 (514)

Centre amical de la Baie
Ville de la Baie, Que.
544-4626 (418)

Centre de dépannage la
passerelle
Alma, Que.
668-4671 (418)

Centre féminin du
Saguenay
Chicoutimi, Que.
549-4343 (418)

Centre refuge Montréal,
Inc.
Montréal, Que.
931-5335 (514)

La passerelle
Amos, Que.
732-9161 (819)

L'Escale de l'Estrie, Inc.
Sherbrooke, Que.
569-6808 (819)

Maison d'accueil Kinsmen
Québec, Que.
688-9024 (418)

Maison d'accueil le Mitan,
Inc.
Ste-Thérèse, Que.
435-7788 (514)

Maison de l'esplanade
Montréal, Que.
845-0151 (514)

Maison Ste-Claire
Montréal, Que.
351-3374 (514)

Maison univers femmes
Touraine, Que.
568-4710 (819)

Résidence de l'avenue A
Trois Rivières, Que.
376-8311 (819)

Toit de l'amitié
La Tuque, Que.
523-4549 (819)

West Island Women's
Shelter
Montréal, Que.
620-4845 (514)

NEW BRUNSWICK

Centre Aide LeRoyer
St-Basile, N.B.
263-5935 (506)

Le Mont Ste-Marie
Edmundston, N.B.
735-3897 (506)

Transition House
Fredericton, N.B.
454-1498 (506)

NOVA SCOTIA

Bryony House
Halifax, N.S.
422-7650 (902)

BIBLIOGRAPHY

Aldridge, James R., et al. "Battered Wives and the Justice System", paper prepared for Dr. John Hogarth, Faculty of Law, University of British Columbia, fall 1978.

Bell, Gerry, "Interspousal Violence - Discovery & Reporting", presented at the second International Conference on Family Law and published in Eekelaar, John M., & Katz, Sanford N., eds., *Family Violence: An International and Interdisciplinary Study*, Butterworths, Toronto, 1978.

Bonenfant, Claire, President, Conseil du statut de la femme, "Des faits connus, une violence cachée," Colloque régional sur la violence, Sept-Îles, Quebec, September 28, 1979.

Chan, Kwok Bun, *Husband-Wife Violence in Toronto*, unpublished Ph.D. thesis, York University, Toronto, 1978.

Coote, Anna & Gill, Tess, *Women's Rights: a Practical Guide*, Penguin, Great Britain, 1977.

Davidson, Terry, *Conjugal Crime: Understanding and Changing the Wife Beating Pattern*, Hawthorn Books, Inc., N.Y. 1970.

Downey, Joanne, & Howell, Jane, *Wife Battering: A Review and Preliminary Enquiry into Local Incidence, Needs and Resources*, United Way of Greater Vancouver, Vancouver, B.C., September 1976.

Dutton, Donald & Levens, Bruce R., (Monograph #2), "Domestic Crisis Intervention: Attitude Survey of Trained and Untrained Police Officers," *Canadian Police College Journal*, Vol. 1, No. 2, Autumn 1977.

Dwyer, Vincent T., "Interspousal Violence: A Response" presented at the second International Conference on Family Law, Montreal, June 13-17, 1977.

Eekelaar, John M., & Katz, Sanford N., eds., *Family Violence: An International and Interdisciplinary Study*, Butterworths, Toronto, 1978.

Epstein, Rachel, Ng, Roxanna, & Trebble, Maggie, *The Social Organization of Family Violence: An Ethnography of Immigrant Experience in Vancouver*. sponsored by the Women's Research Center, Vancouver, B.C., 1978.

Errington, Gene, "Family Violence - Is It a Woman's Problem?" Speech given at the Symposium on Family Violence, Vancouver, B.C., March 1977.

Field, Martha H. & Henry Γ., "Marital Violence and the Criminal Process: Neither Justice nor Peace", *Social Service Review*, 47 (2), 1973, pp. 221-240.

Fields, Marjory D., "Representing Battered Wives, or What to Do Until the Police Arrive", *The Family Law Reporter*, Monograph # 25, April 5, 1977, p. 3.

Freeman, Michael, D.A. "Le vice anglais? - Wife Battering in English and American Law" in *Family Law Quarterly*, Vol. XI, #3, Fall 1977.

Friedan, Betty, "Feminism Takes a New Turn" in *New York Times Magazine*, November 1979

Gelles, Richard J., *The Violent Home: A Study of Physical Aggression Between Husbands and Wives*, Sage, Beverly Hills, California, 1972.

Goldman, Pearl, *Violence Against Women in the Family*, Institute of Comparative Law, McGill University, unpublished Master of Laws thesis, 1978.

Gropper, Arlene, & Marvin, Joyce, "Violence Begins at Home," *The Canadian*, Saturday, November 20, 1976.

Hamlin, Diane, *The Nature and Extent of Spouse Assault*, Center for Women Policy Studies, Clearinghouse Director, Washington, D.C., October 1978.

Hayden, Joyce, "Wife Battering - One Perspective," Data from the first year's operation of Vernon Transition House, Vernon, B.C., August 1, 1977 - July 31, 1978.

Hilberman, Elaine, M.D. & Munson, Kit, B.S.W., "60 Battered Women: A Preliminary Report" prepared for special session - *Battered Women - Culture as Destiny*, American Psych. Association Meetings, Toronto, Ontario, May 5, 1977.

de Koninck, Maria, *Réflexion sur la condition des femmes violentées*, Conseil du statut de la femme, Quebec, June 1977.

Langley, Robert & Levy, Richard C., *Wife Beating: The Silent Crisis*, Pocket Books, N.Y., 1977.

Larouche, Ginette, "Les femmes violentées", paper for "Etudes thématiques I", graduate studies, Université de Montréal, June 1979.

Leveille, Sandra, "Violence Against Women: Social Order - Social Change", unpublished, University of Manitoba, April 1978.

Levens, Bruce & Dutton, Donald, United Way of Greater Vancouver, "Domestic Crisis Intervention: Citizens' Request for Service and the Vancouver Police Department's Response", (Monograph #1) *Canadian Police College Journal*, Summer 1977.

Levens, Bruce R., "Domestic Crisis Intervention: A Literature Review of Domestic Dispute Intervention Programs - July, 1977 (Monograph #3) *Canadian Police College Journal*, Volume 2, #2; Volume 3, #3, 1978.

Levens, Bruce R., United Way of Greater Vancouver, "Domestic Crisis Intervention: Domestic Disputes, Police Response and Social Agency Referral" (Monograph #4), *Canadian Police College Journal*, Vol. 2, #4, 1978.

Levens, Bruce R., United Way of Greater Vancouver, "The Social Service Role of Police in Domestic Crisis Intervention" (Monograph #5), unpublished, 1978.

Levine, Helen, "On the Framework of Women's Lives and Feminist Counselling", presented at Counselling for Women workshop, Moncton, N.B., September 1978. Revised December 1978.

Martin, Del, *Battered Wives*, Pocket Books, New York, 1977.

Martin, Del, "Battered Women: Society's Problem", in Chapman, J.R., & Gates, M., eds., *The Victimization of Women*, Sage, Beverly Hills, 1978.

Martin, J.P., ed. *Violence and the Family*, John Wiley and Sons, New York, 1978.

McFadyen, Joanna L., "Inter-Spousal Rape: The Need for Law Reform", in Eekelaar & Katz, eds., *Family Violence*, Butterworths, Toronto, 1978.

McKay, Robin, *A Handbook on Domestic Assaults*, Commissioned by Kingston Interval House, Box 224, Kingston, Ontario, 1977.

MacLeod, Flora (Ed.), *Family Violence: Report of the Task Force on Family Violence*, United Way of the Lower Mainland, Vancouver, B.C., May 1979.

Menzies, Ken, *The Women's Emergency Centre: An Assessment*, Department of Sociology and Anthropology, University of Guelph, 1977.

Metzger, Mary, "A Social History of Battered Women." Copies distributed at consultation for Feminist Services Training Programme Coordinators, sponsored by Secretary of State Women's Programme, Nov. 28-30, 1979.

New Woman Center Journal, "The Situation of the Battered Woman" Vol. 1, #2, October 1977.

Nourry, Simone, *Essai sur la condition de la femme violentée*, unpublished thesis, Faculty of Social Sciences, University of Sherbrooke.

Ostrowski, Margaret V., *Legal Process for Battered Women*, United Way of the Lower Mainland, Vancouver, B.C., June 1979.

Pizzey, Erin, *Scream Quietly or the Neighbours Will Hear*, Penguin Books, Harmondsworth, England, 1974.

Prescott, James W., "Body Pleasure and the Origins of Violence", *The Futurist*, April 1975.

Schlachet, Barbara Cohn, "Rapid Intervention with Families in Crisis in a Court Setting", in Eekelaar & Katz, eds., *Family Violence: An International and Interdisciplinary Study*, Butterworths, Toronto, 1978.

Shee, Sandra, & Deragon, Sylvie, "Le problème de la femme maltraitée au Québec" in D'Oyley, Vincent, ed., *Domestic Violence: Issues & Dynamics*, Ontario Institute for Studies in Education, Information Series #7, Toronto, 1978, pp. 169-180.

Small, Shirley Endicott, "Wife Assault: An Overview of the Problem in Canada", Support Services for Assaulted Women, Toronto, 1979.

Smith, Dorothy E., "A Sociology for Women", in Sherman, Julia A., & Torton Beck, Evelyn, eds., *The Prism of Sex: Essays in the Sociology of Knowledge*, University of Wisconsin Press, Madison, 1979.

Smith, Dorothy E., "Women and the Politics of Professionalism" unpublished, Ottawa, 1978.

Smith, Dorothy E., "Women's Inequality and the Family" unpublished, Ottawa, 1978.

Statistics Canada, *Homicide in Canada: A Statistical Synopsis*, Cat. #85-505E, Occ.

Steinmetz, Suzanne K., *The Cycle of Violence: Assertive, Aggressive and Abusive Family Interaction*, Praeger Publishers, New York, 1977.

Steinmetz, S.K. & Strauss, M.A., eds., *Violence in the Family*, Dodd, Mead & Company, New York, 1975.

Strauss, Murray A., "Wife Beating: How Common and Why", in Eekelaar & Katz, eds., *Family Violence*.

Support Services for Assaulted Women, *Wife Assault in Canada - a Fact Sheet*, available from P.O. Box 245, Station "K", Toronto, Ontario M4P 2G5.

Van Den Berghe, Pierre L., "Bringing Beasts Back In: Toward a Biosocial Theory of Aggression", *American Sociological Review*, Vol. 39, December 1974, pp. 777-788.

Van Stolk, Mary, "A Harder Look at Domestic Violence", *RCMP Gazette*, fall 1978.

Women in Transition, a Canada Works Project, Thunder Bay, Ontario, 1978.

Conferences:

Domestic Violence Between Mates: Issues and Dynamics, Information Series #7. Proceedings of "Domestic Violence Between Mates: Couples in Conflict", Ontario Institute for Studies in Education, Toronto, Ontario, March 11-12, 1977.

Eekelaar, John M., & Katz, Sanford N., eds., *Family Violence: An International and Interdisciplinary Study*. Proceedings of the second International Conference on Family Law, Montreal, June 1977. Butterworths, Scarborough, Ontario, 1978.

Symposium on Family Violence. Vancouver, B.C., March 9-11, 1977. Report of the Proceedings published by United Way of Greater Vancouver, Vancouver, B.C., 1977.

Workshop on Violence in Canadian Society. University of Toronto, Centre of Criminology, 1975. Report of the Proceedings published by the Centre of Criminology, Toronto, 1975.

Publications of the Canadian Advisory Council on the Status of Women

Les publications suivantes sont également disponibles en français.

Birth Planning

Background Notes on Birth Planning and Conception Control by Mary Pearson, June 1979.

A Statement on Birth Planning, CACSW Recommendations, September 1976.

Abortion in Canada: Background Notes on the Proposed Amendments to the Criminal Code by Louise Dulude, November 1975.

Notes on the Law of Birth Planning in Canada by Henri Major, August 1975.

The Family

One-Parent Family CACSW Principles and Recommendations, January 1977.

New Directions for Public Policy: A Position Paper on the One-Parent Family by S. June Menzies, April 1976.

Background Notes on the Federal Law Reform Commission's Working Paper, "The Family Court" by Henri Major, June 1974.

Financial Status of Women

CACSW Annotated Recommendations on Women and Taxation, January 1978.

Background Notes on Proposed Amendments to the CPP (Bill C-49) by Henri Major, June 1977.

Marital Issues

Statement on Matrimonial Property Laws in Canada, February 1979.
Divorce Law Reform, CACSW Recommendations, September 1976.
Study Paper on Divorce by Marcia H. Rioux, June 1976.
A Definition of Equity in Marriage, CACSW Statement of Principle, May 1976.
Notes on Selected Federal Statutes Recognizing Common-Law Relationships by Henri Major, July 1975.

Rape and Sexual Offences

Recommendations of the CACSW on Bill C-51, an Act to Amend the Criminal Code, the Canada Evidence Act and the Parole Act, October 1978.
Background Notes on the Proposed Amendments to the Criminal Code in Respect of Indecent Assault (Bill C-52) by Marcia H. Rioux and Joanna L. McFadyen and Recommendations of the CACSW, June 1978.
Rape and Sexual Assault, Person Papers, December 1976.
Wife battering in Canada by Linda MacLeod, assisted by Andrée Cadieux, January 1980.

Social Policy and Issues

Women and Aging: A Report on the Rest of our Lives by Louise Dulude, April 1978.
Indian Women and the Law in Canada: Citizens Minus by Kathleen Jamieson, April 1978.
Women and Aging (Fact Sheet no. 2), October 1979.

Women and Work

The Second Time Around: A Study of Women Returning to the Work Force by Mary Pearson, April 1979.
Problems of Immigrant Women in the Canadian Labour Force by Sheila McLeod Arnopoulos, January 1979.
Five Million Women: A Study of the Canadian Housewife by Monique Proulx, June 1978.
Health Hazards at Work, Person Papers, January 1977.
Occupational Health Hazards to Women: A Synoptic View by Ann George, January 1977.
Women and Work (Fact Sheet no. 1), June 1979.

The Federal Government

Women in the Public Service: Barriers to Equal Opportunity, February 1979.

General

The Status of Women and the CBC - A brief by the CACSW to the CRTC, November 1978.
Recommendations of the CACSW by subject, October 1978.
Sharing the Power, a kit prepared by CACSW members, April 1978.
Canadian Perspective on Sex Stereotyping in Advertising by Alice E. Courtney and Thomas W. Whipple, June 1978.
International Decade for Women: 1976-1985: What It Means to Canadian Women by Mary Pearson, November 1977.
Annual Report of the Canadian Advisory Council on the Status of Women.
Ten Years Later - assessment of the Federal Government's implementation of R.C.S.W. recommendations, October 1979.